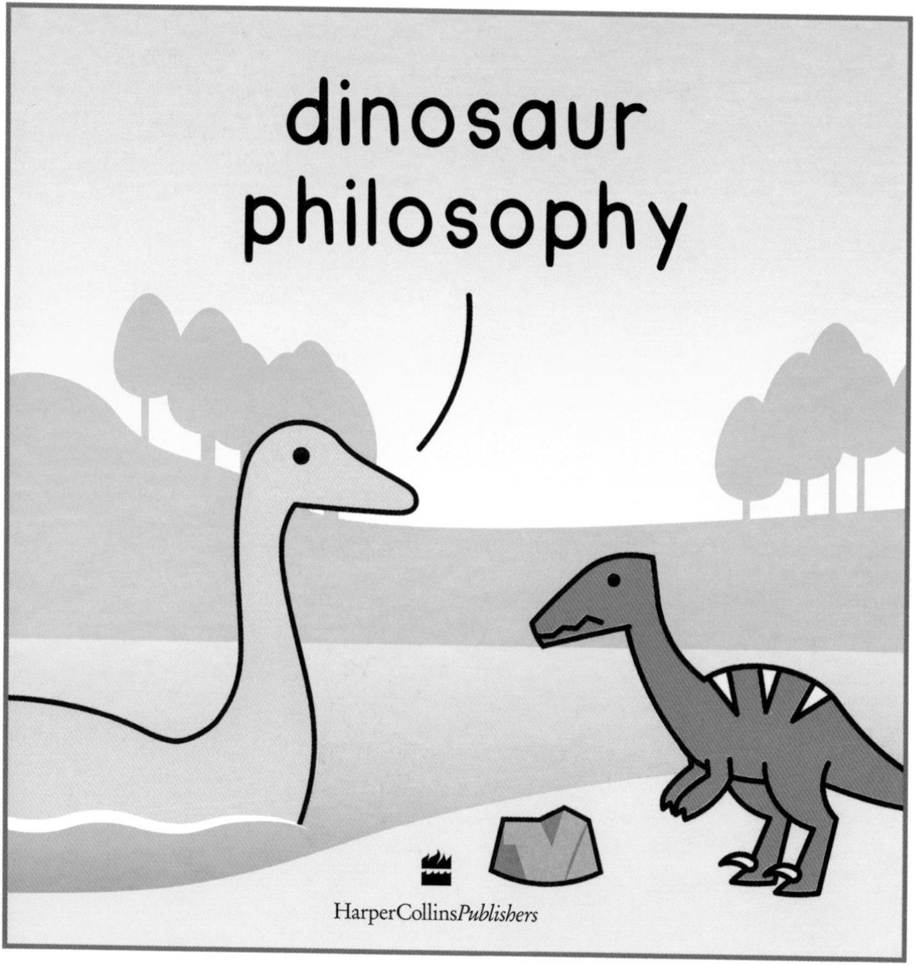
dinosaur
philosophy
HarperCollinsPublishers

HarperCollins*Publishers*
1 London Bridge Street
London SE1 9GF

www.harpercollins.co.uk

HarperCollins*Publishers*
1st Floor, Watermarque Building, Ringsend Road
Dublin 4, Ireland

First published by HarperCollins*Publishers* 2022

1 3 5 7 9 10 8 6 4 2

Text © James Stewart 2022
Illustrations © K Roméy 2022

Hey Buddy Comics assert the moral right to be
identified as the authors of this work

A catalogue record of this book is
available from the British Library

ISBN 978-0-00-853084-6

Printed and bound in Latvia

MIX
Paper from
responsible sources
FSC **FSC™ C007454**
www.fsc.org

This book is produced from independently certified FSC™ paper to
ensure responsible forest management.

For more information visit: *www.harpercollins.co.uk/green*

contents

To Nina,
Oliver, Ada and
Penny. My forever pack.
James

To L, KC, Jack and Caven
for being my motivation
to get out of bed.
K

introduction

In the introduction to our first book, *dinosaur therapy*, I said I thought that the loneliness, depression and anxiety caused by the COVID-19 pandemic were part of the reason why our mental-health-focused dinosaur comics took off so quickly. As I write this a year later and the pandemic continues, I do not think these issues are becoming the new normal; rather, I think they were always normal, and the pandemic has merely caused an increase both in their incidence and our need to talk about them. Every year more people live their lives with some kind of mental-health issue hanging over them. I hope that talking about these issues in a blunt and open way offers those people some brief catharsis.

dinosaur philosophy

While there are some comics in this book that touch on specific philosophical issues, in general they focus on philosophy in the sense of one's attitudes towards, and principles about, life. If I had to sum up briefly the dinosaur philosophy, I would do so thus:

Face the negatives in life with hope and a sense of humour. Welcome the positive sides of life without cynicism and with an open heart. Remember that however annoying and frustrating people might sometimes seem, they are all we have.*

I regularly fail to live up to these principles, but what kind of principles would they be if they were easy to follow? On that positive note, enjoy the comics!

James

*Okay, we also have dogs.

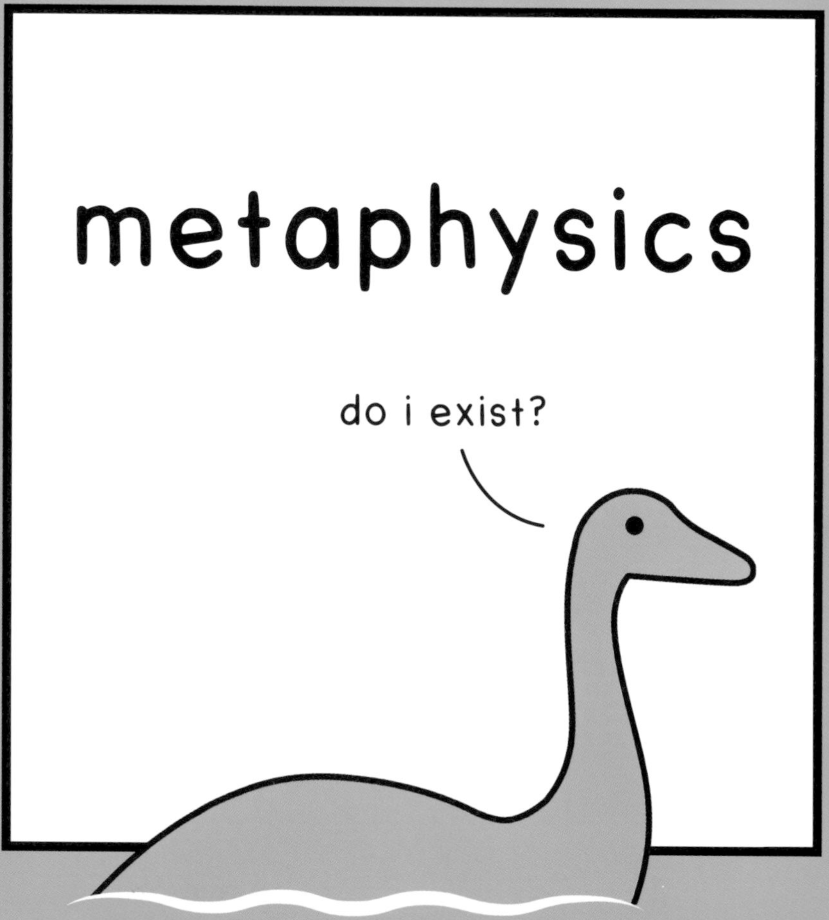
metaphysics
do i exist?

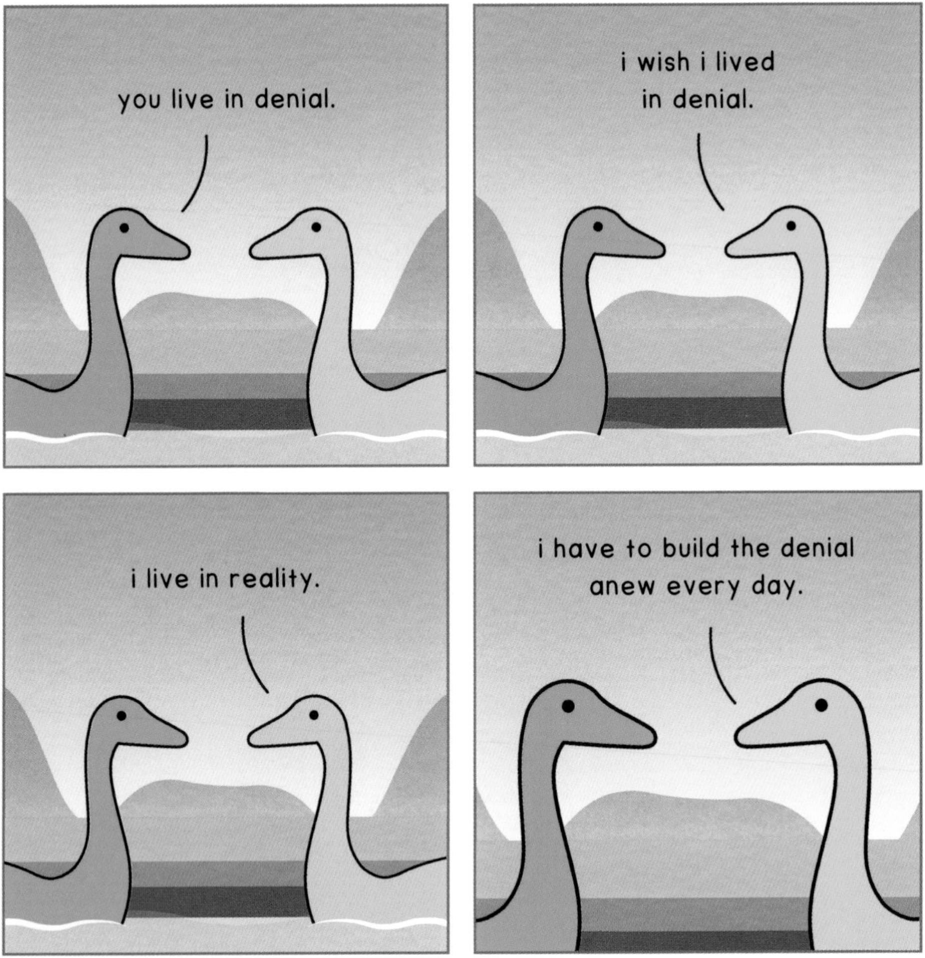
you live in denial.
i wish i lived in denial.
i live in reality.
i have to build the denial anew every day.

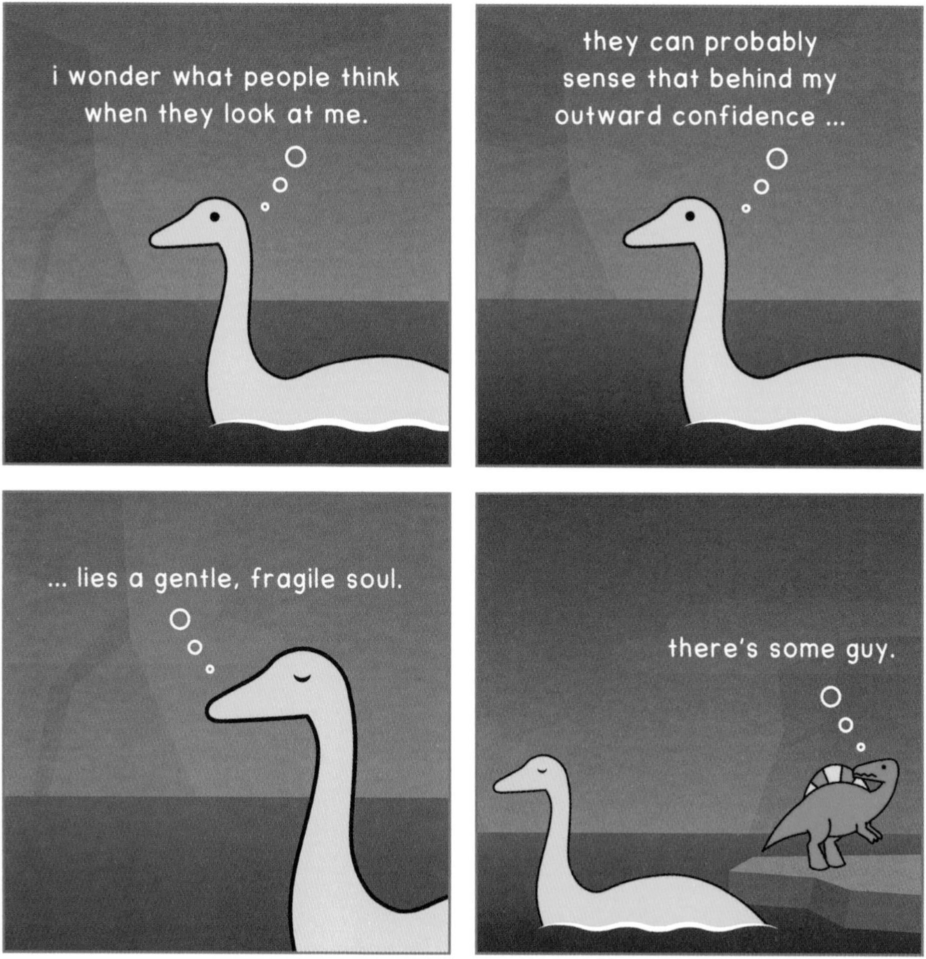
i wonder what people think when they look at me.
they can probably sense that behind my outward confidence ...
... lies a gentle, fragile soul.
there's some guy.

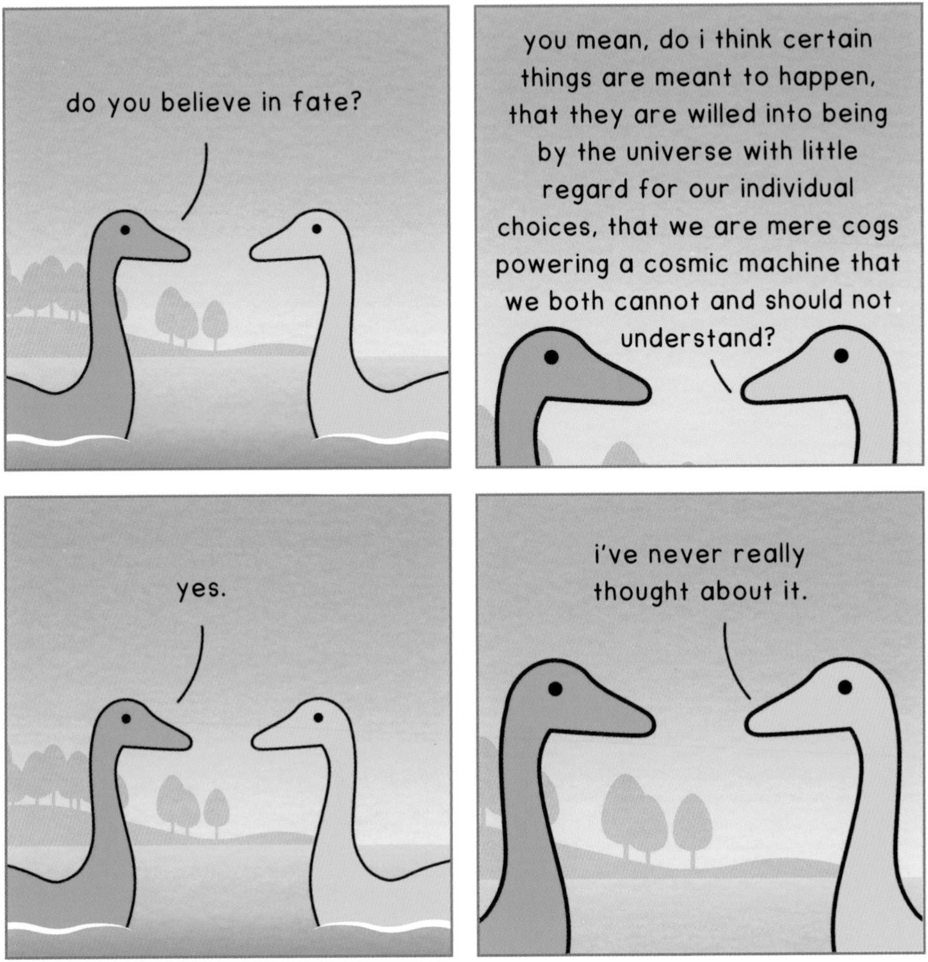
do you believe in fate?
you mean, do i think certain things are meant to happen, that they are willed into being by the universe with little regard for our individual choices, that we are mere cogs powering a cosmic machine that we both cannot and should not understand?
yes.
i've never really thought about it.

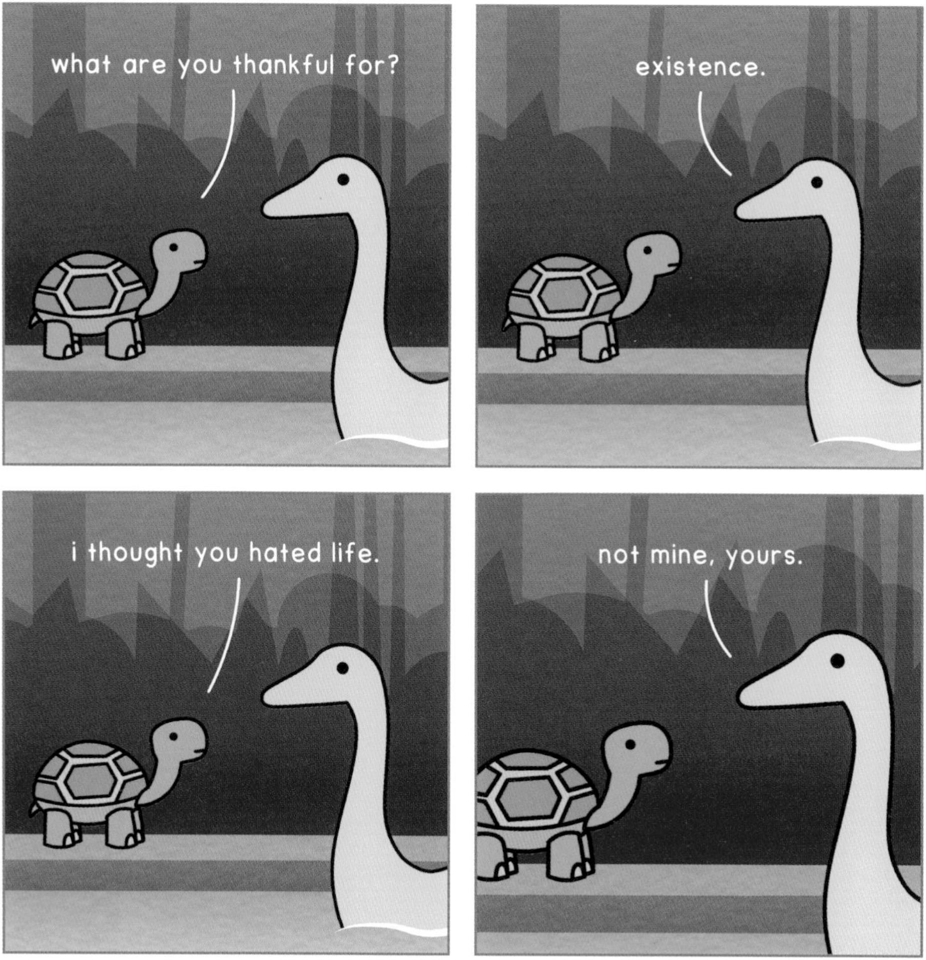
what are you thankful for?
existence.
i thought you hated life.
not mine, yours.

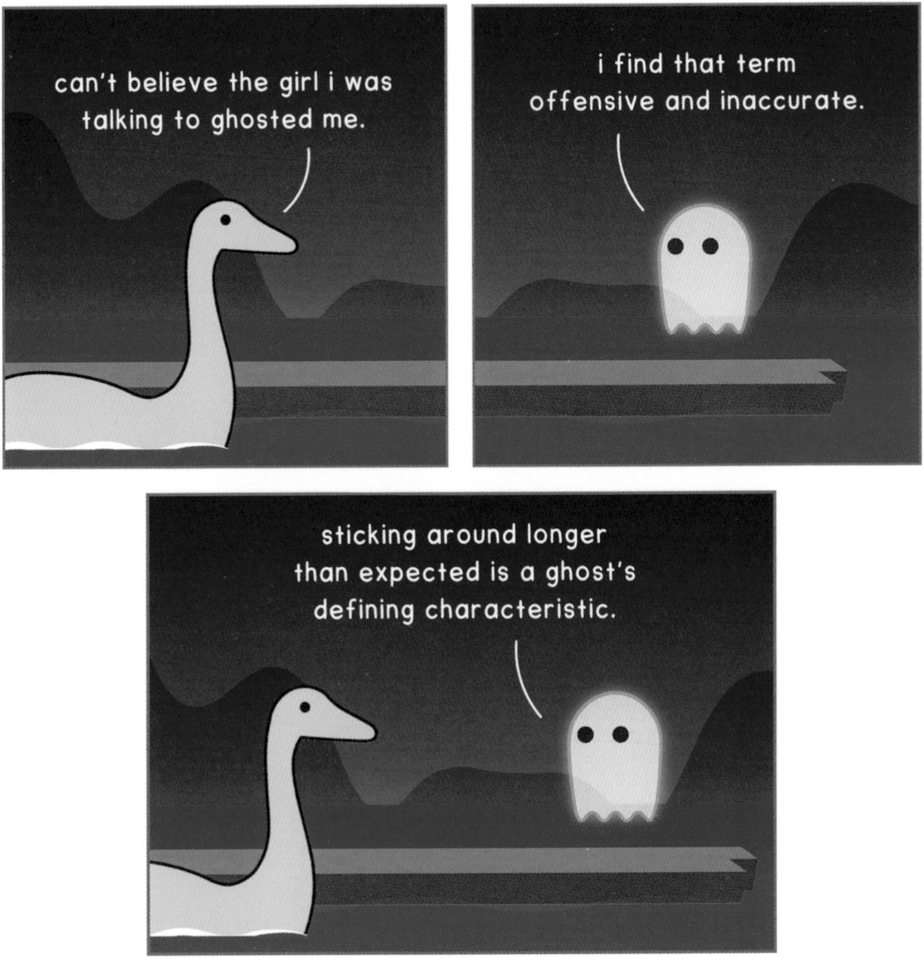
can't believe the girl i was talking to ghosted me.
i find that term offensive and inaccurate.
sticking around longer than expected is a ghost's defining characteristic.

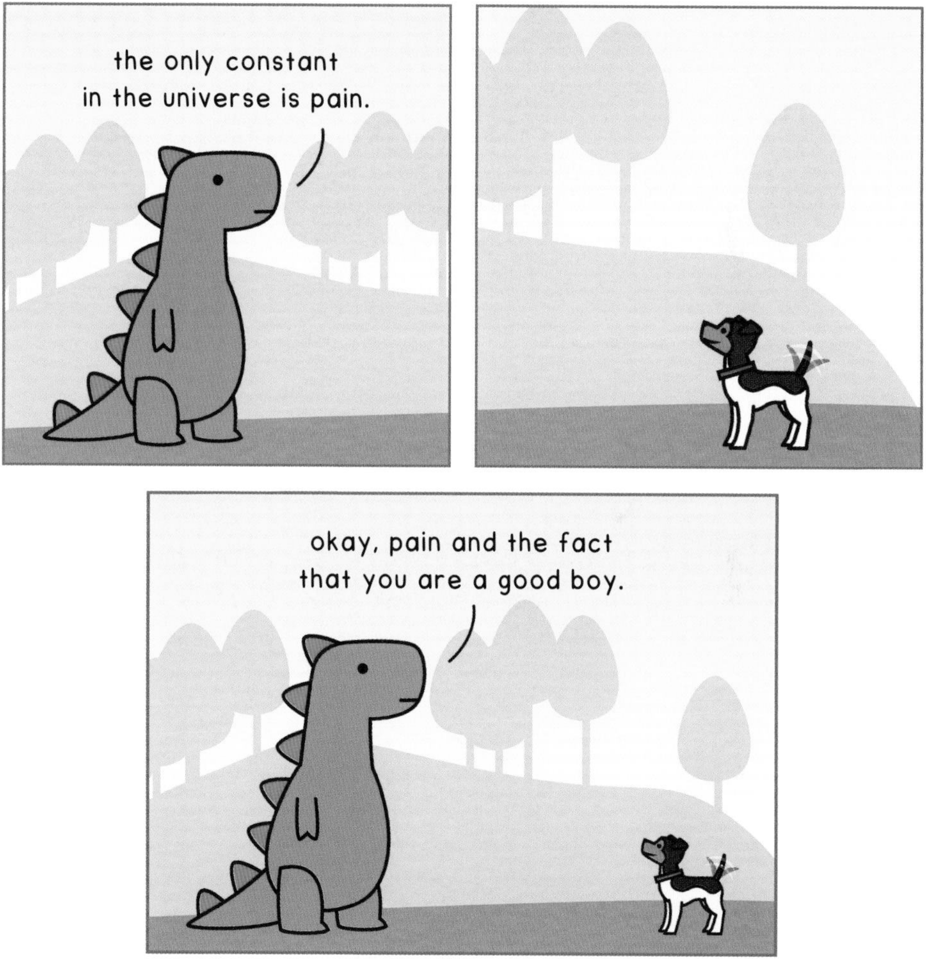
the only constant
in the universe is pain.
okay, pain and the fact
that you are a good boy.

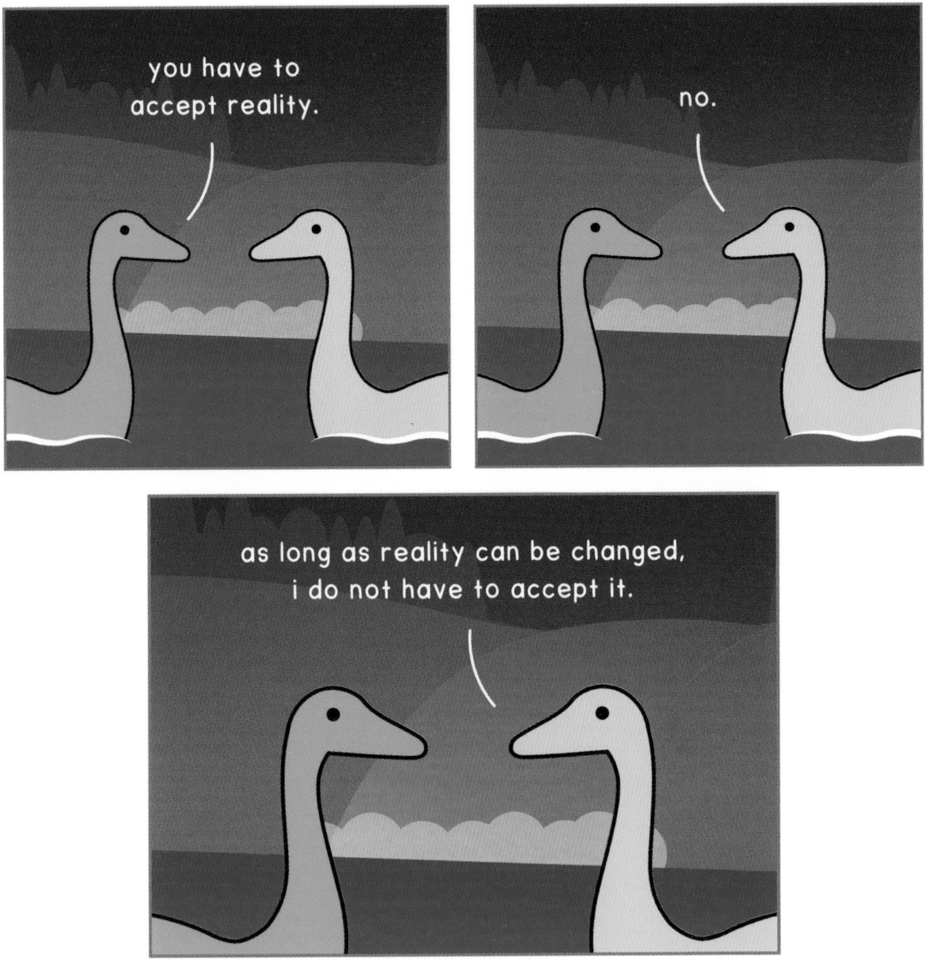
you have to accept reality.
no.
as long as reality can be changed, i do not have to accept it.

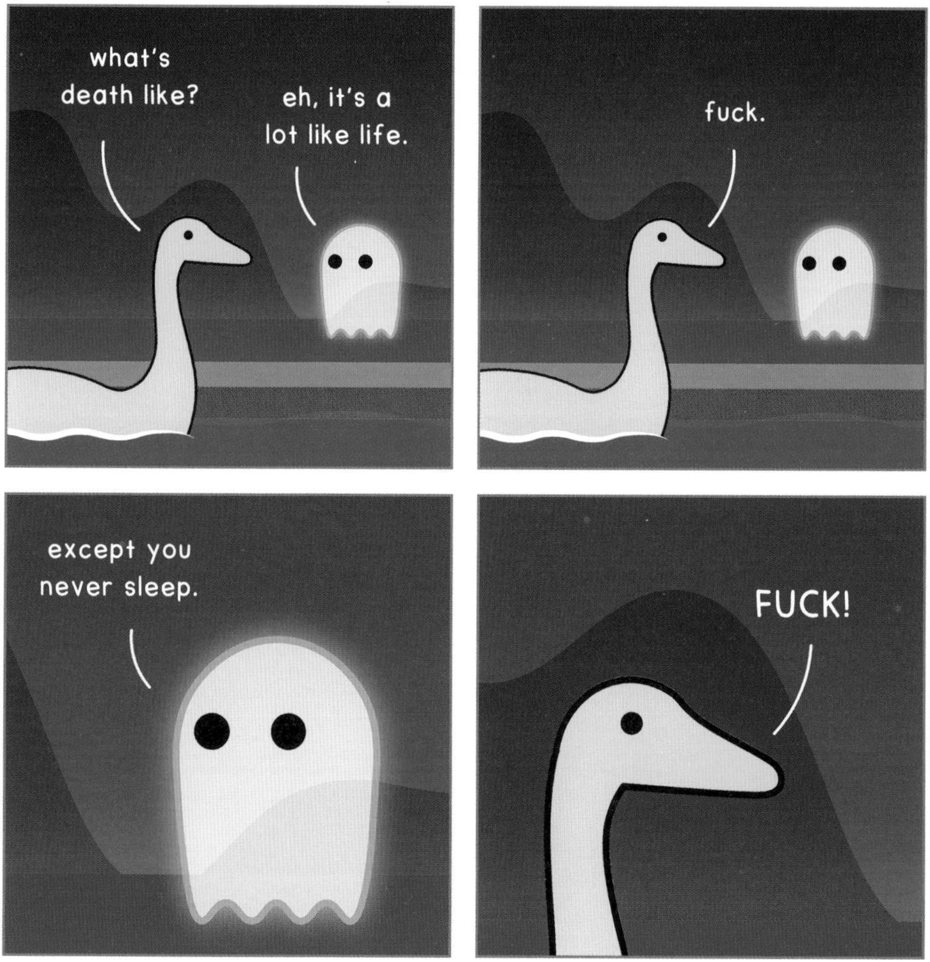
what's death like?
eh, it's a lot like life.
fuck.
except you never sleep.
FUCK!

epistemology

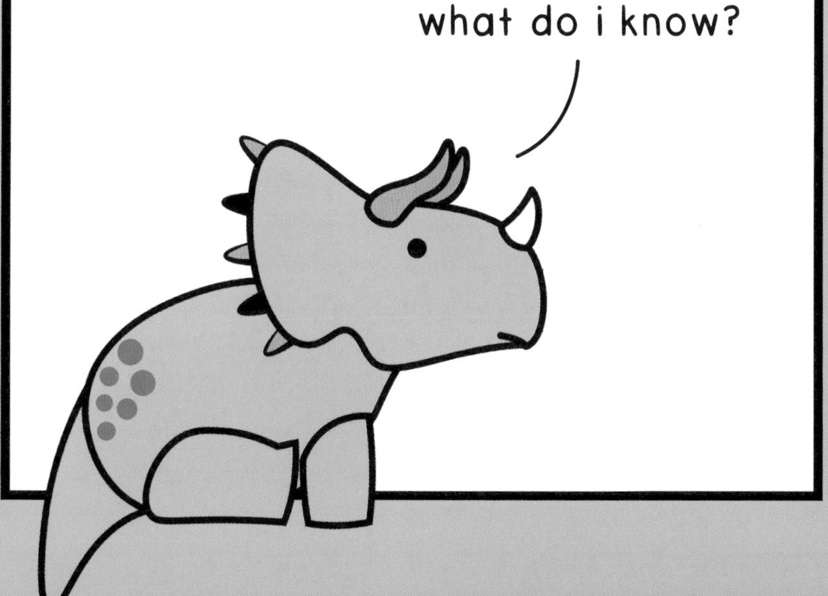
what do i know?

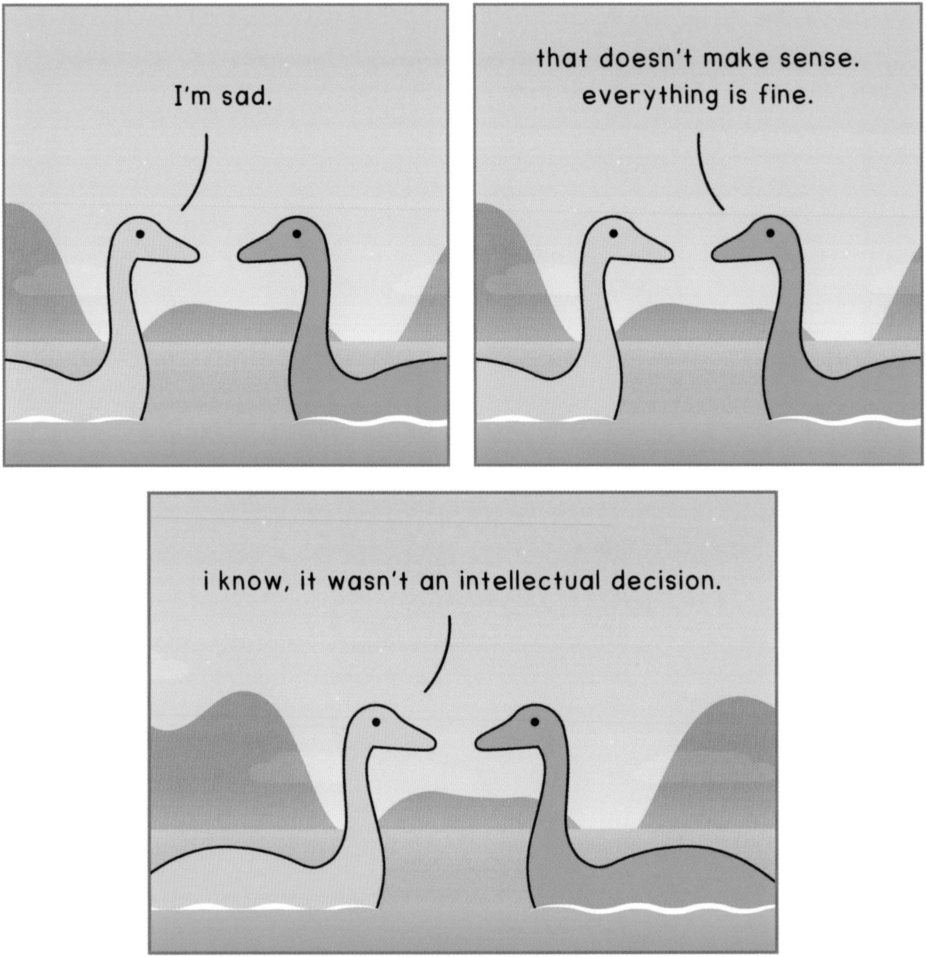
I'm sad.
that doesn't make sense. everything is fine.
i know, it wasn't an intellectual decision.

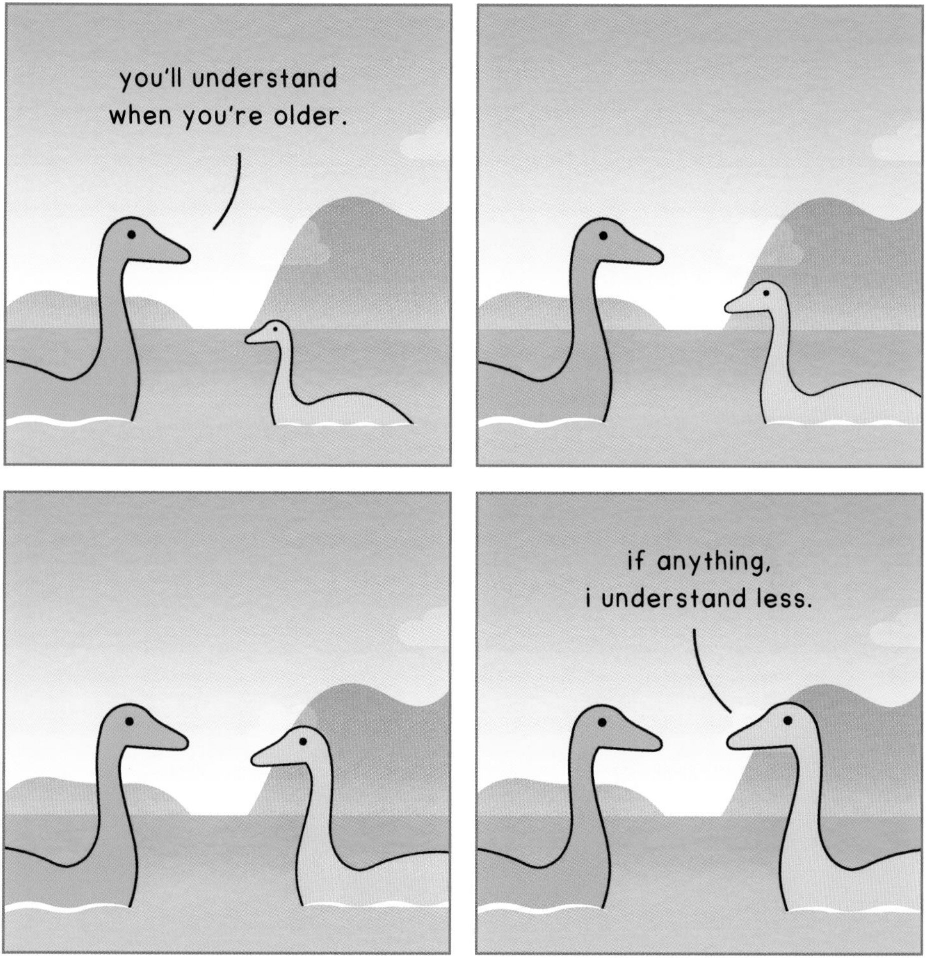
you'll understand
when you're older.
if anything,
i understand less.

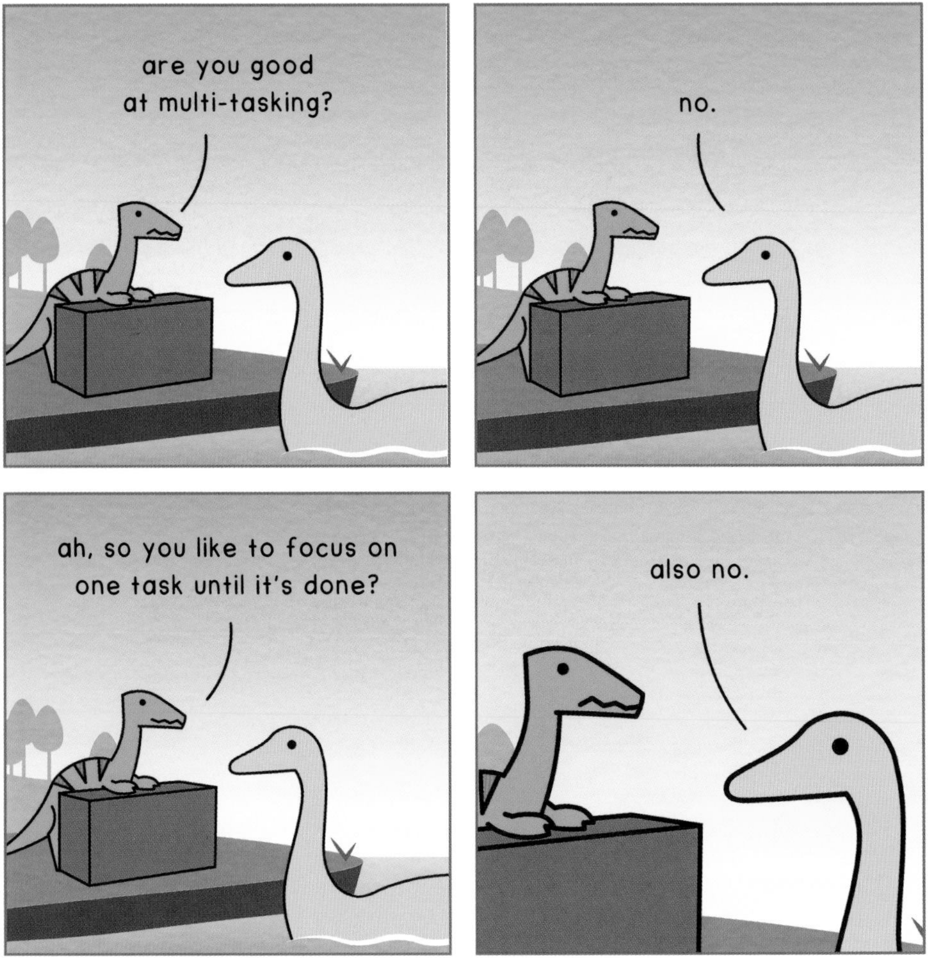
are you good at multi-tasking?
no.
ah, so you like to focus on one task until it's done?
also no.

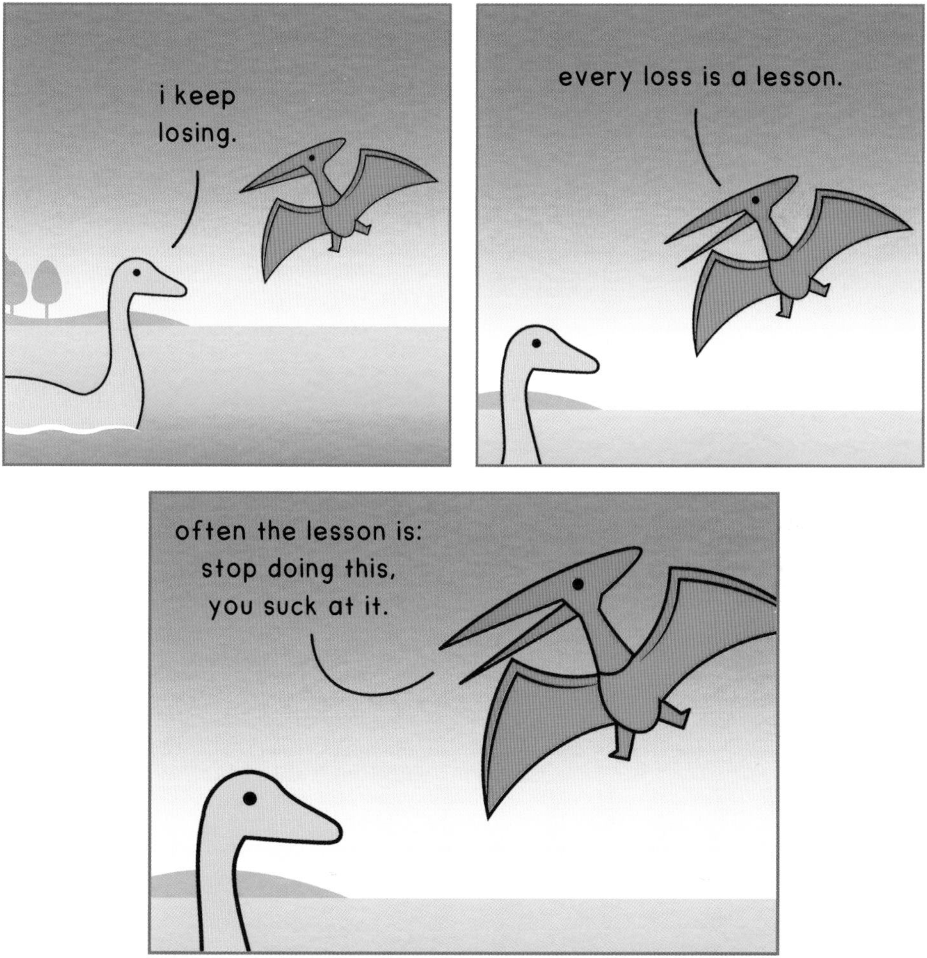

i keep losing.
every loss is a lesson.
often the lesson is: stop doing this, you suck at it.

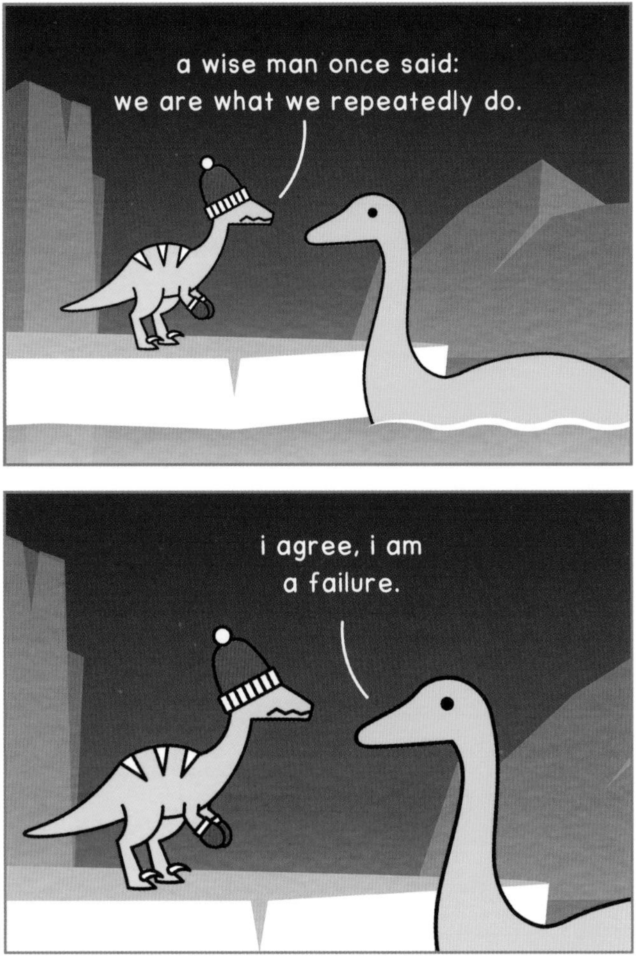
a wise man once said:
we are what we repeatedly do.
i agree, i am
a failure.

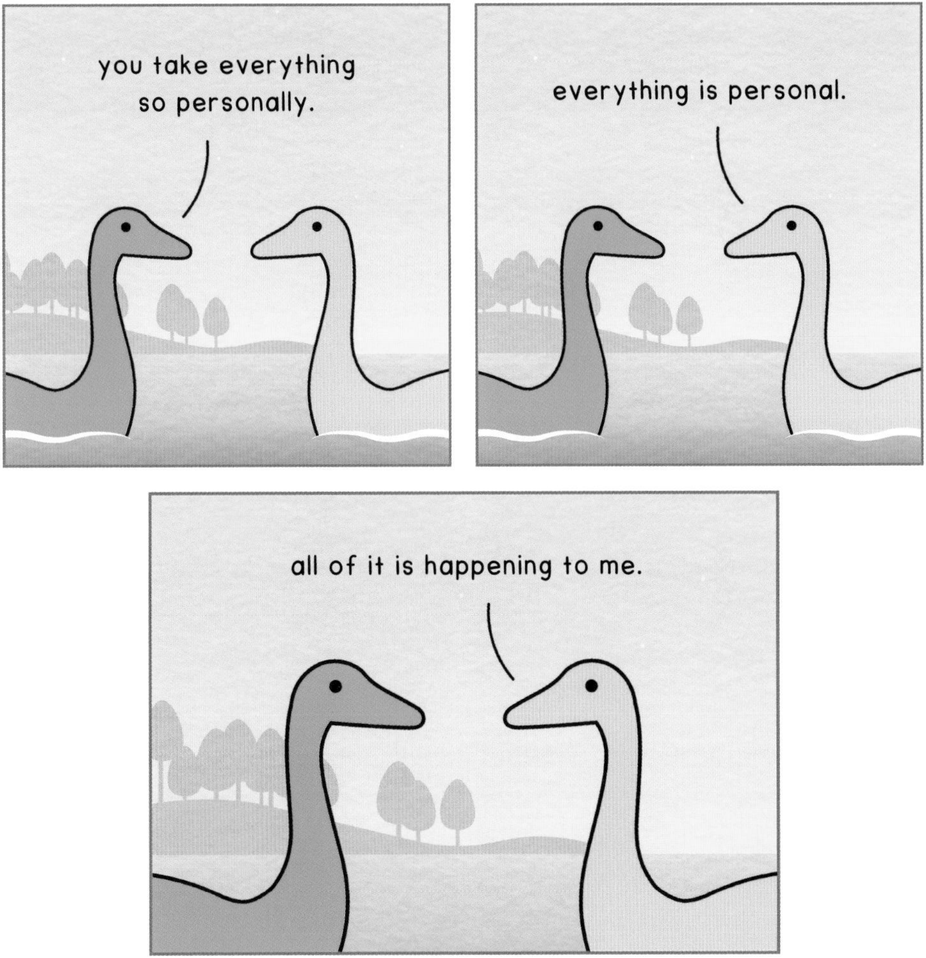
you take everything so personally.
everything is personal.
all of it is happening to me.

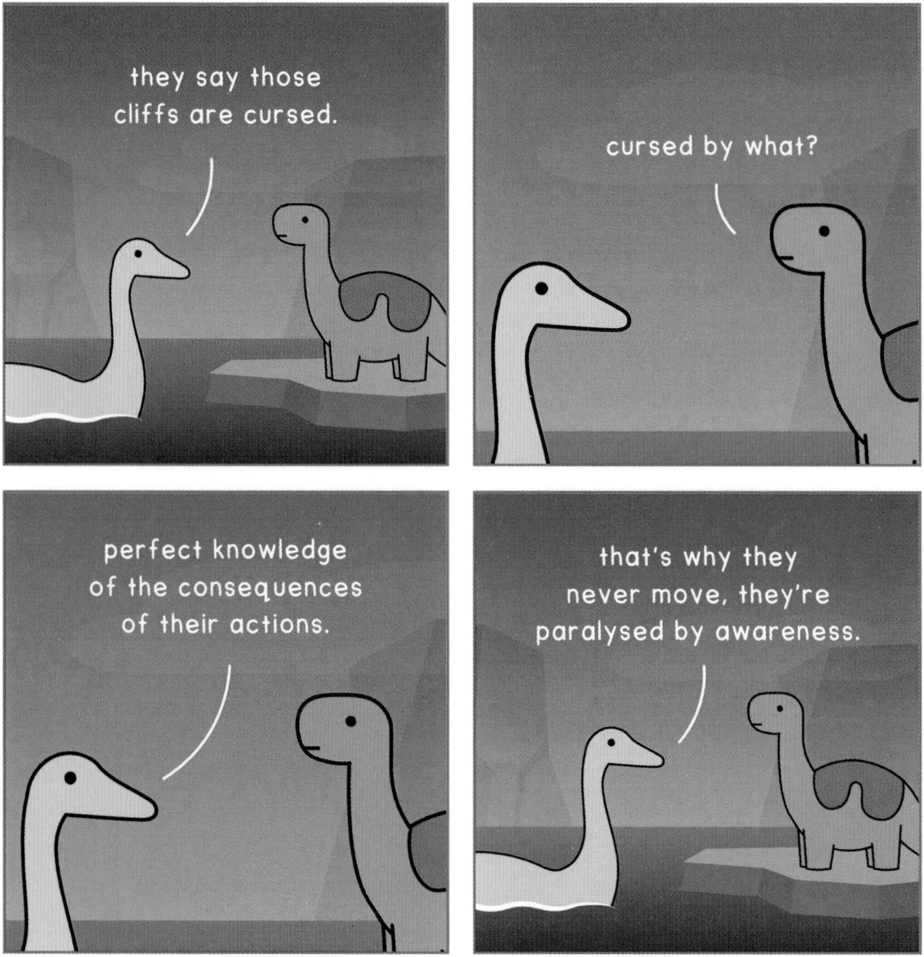
they say those cliffs are cursed.
cursed by what?
perfect knowledge of the consequences of their actions.
that's why they never move, they're paralysed by awareness.

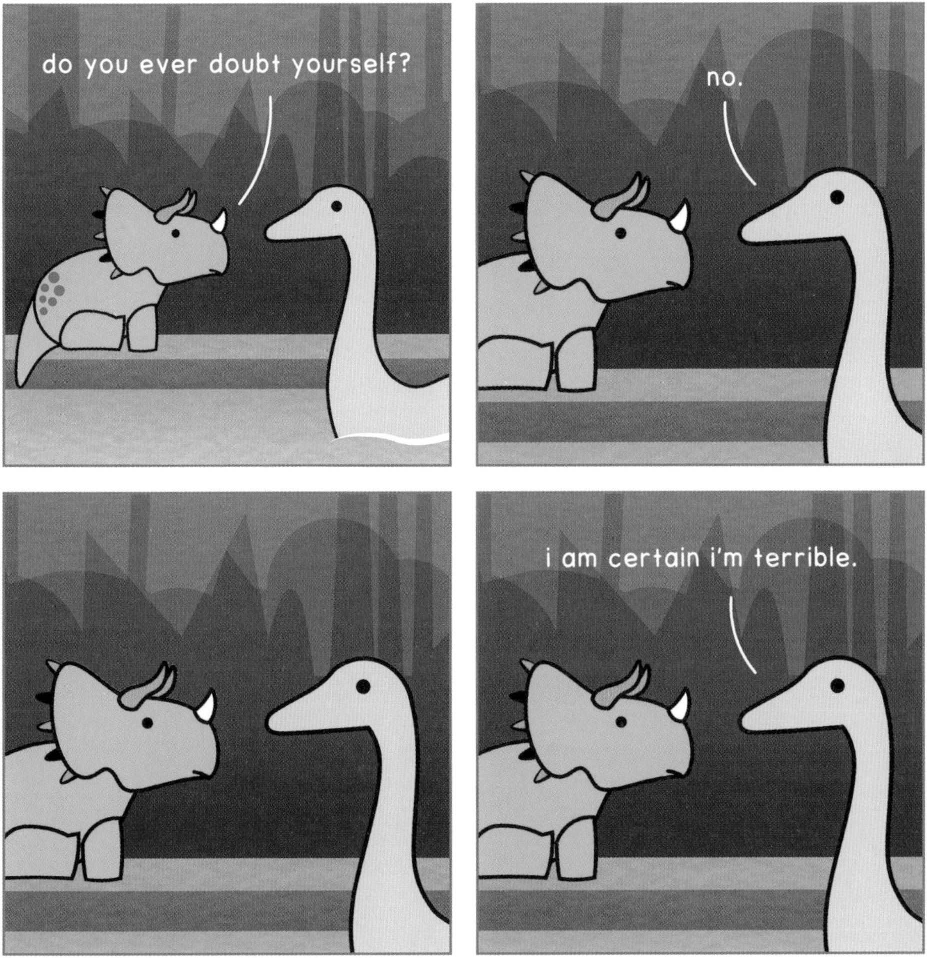
do you ever doubt yourself?
no.
i am certain i'm terrible.

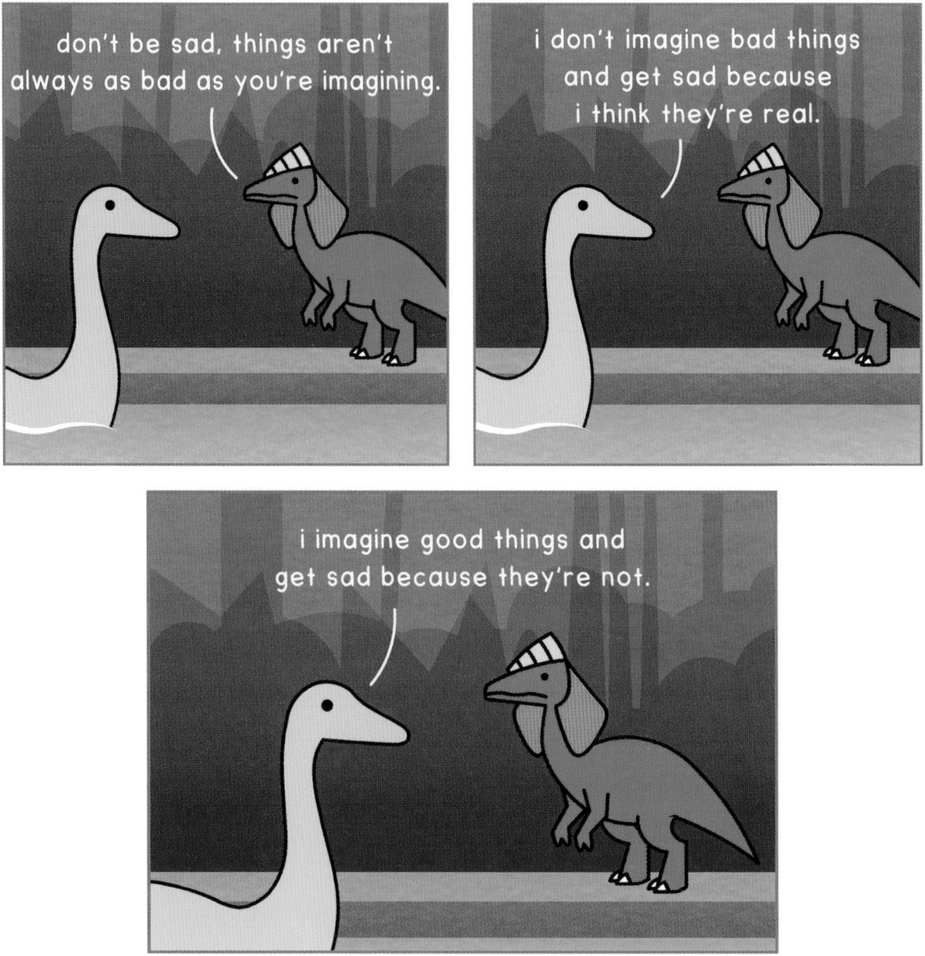

don't be sad, things aren't always as bad as you're imagining.
i don't imagine bad things and get sad because i think they're real.
i imagine good things and get sad because they're not.

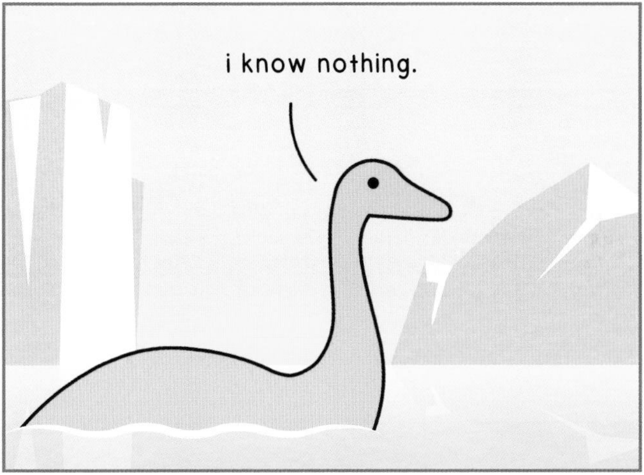
i know nothing.
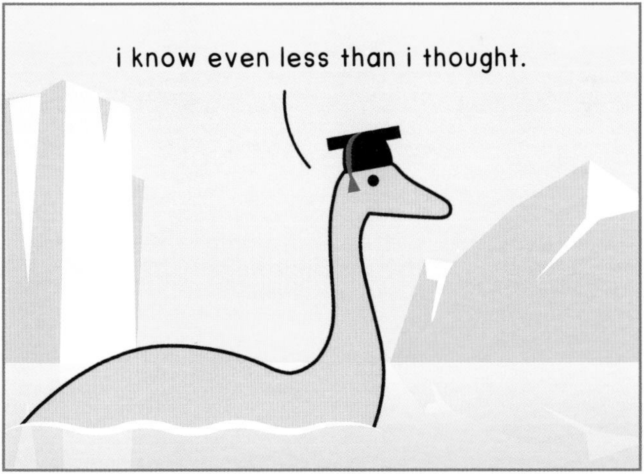
i know even less than i thought.

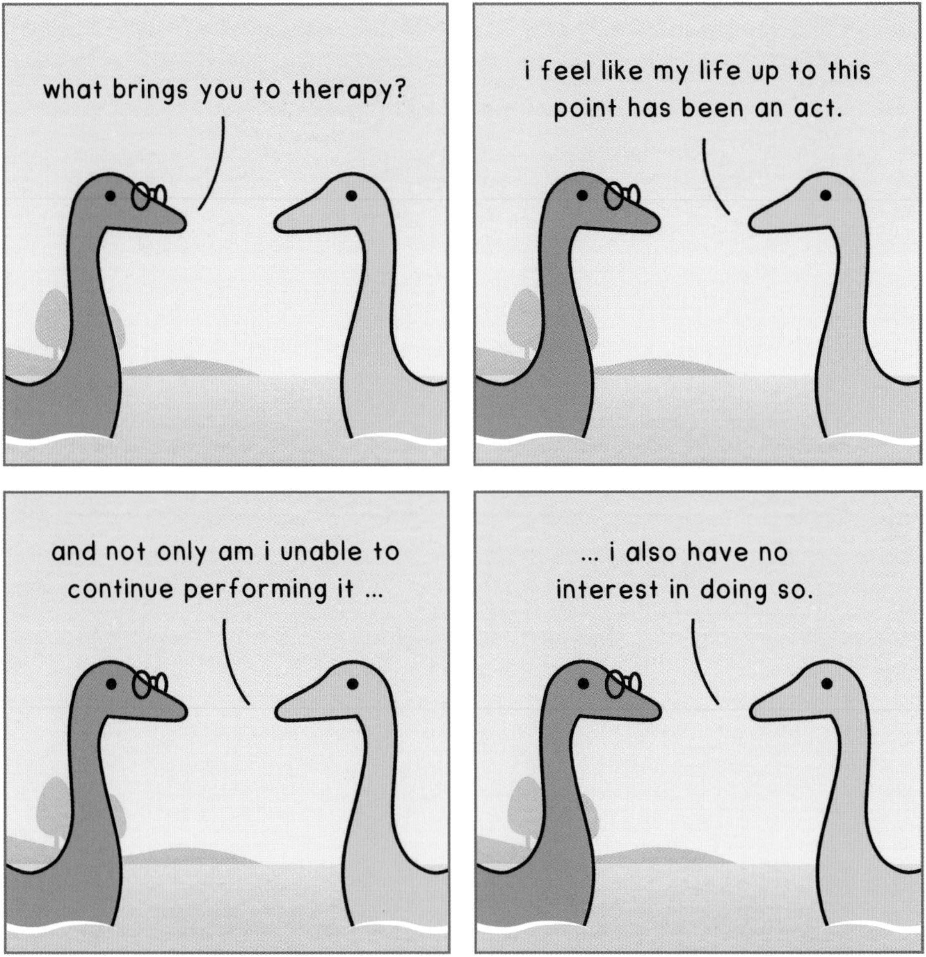
what brings you to therapy?
i feel like my life up to this point has been an act.
and not only am i unable to continue performing it ...
... i also have no interest in doing so.

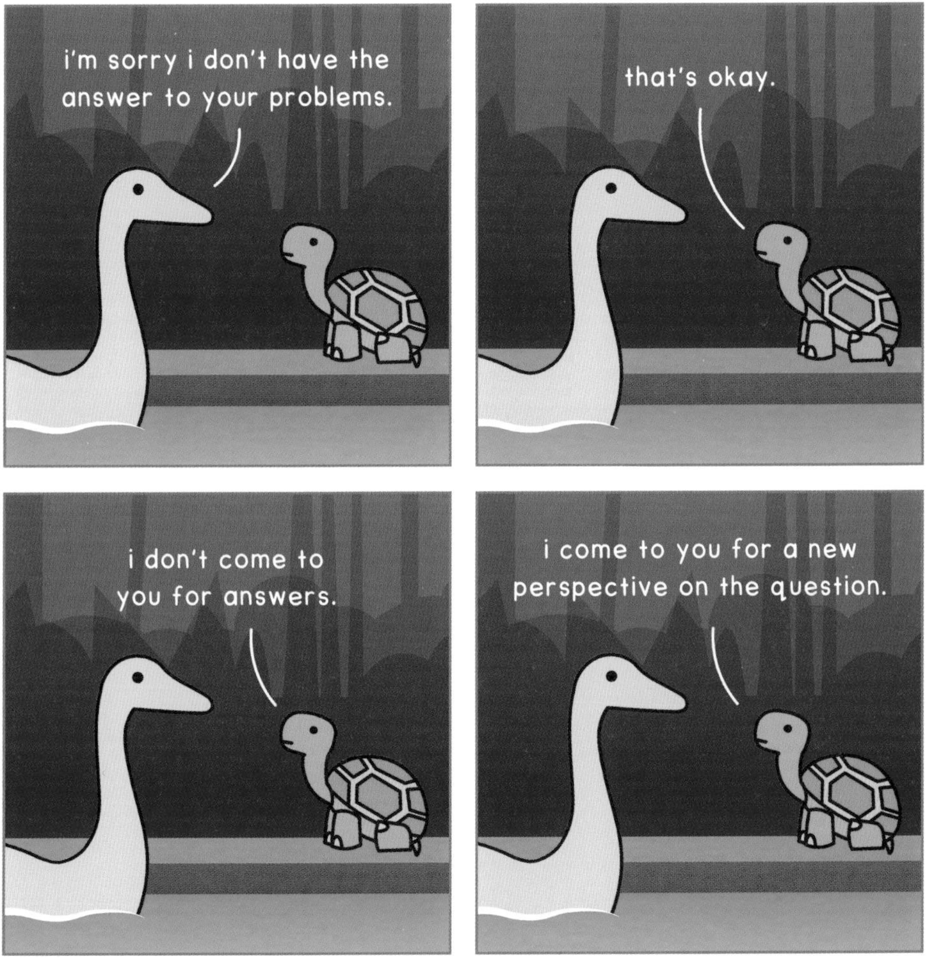
i'm sorry i don't have the answer to your problems.
that's okay.
i don't come to you for answers.
i come to you for a new perspective on the question.

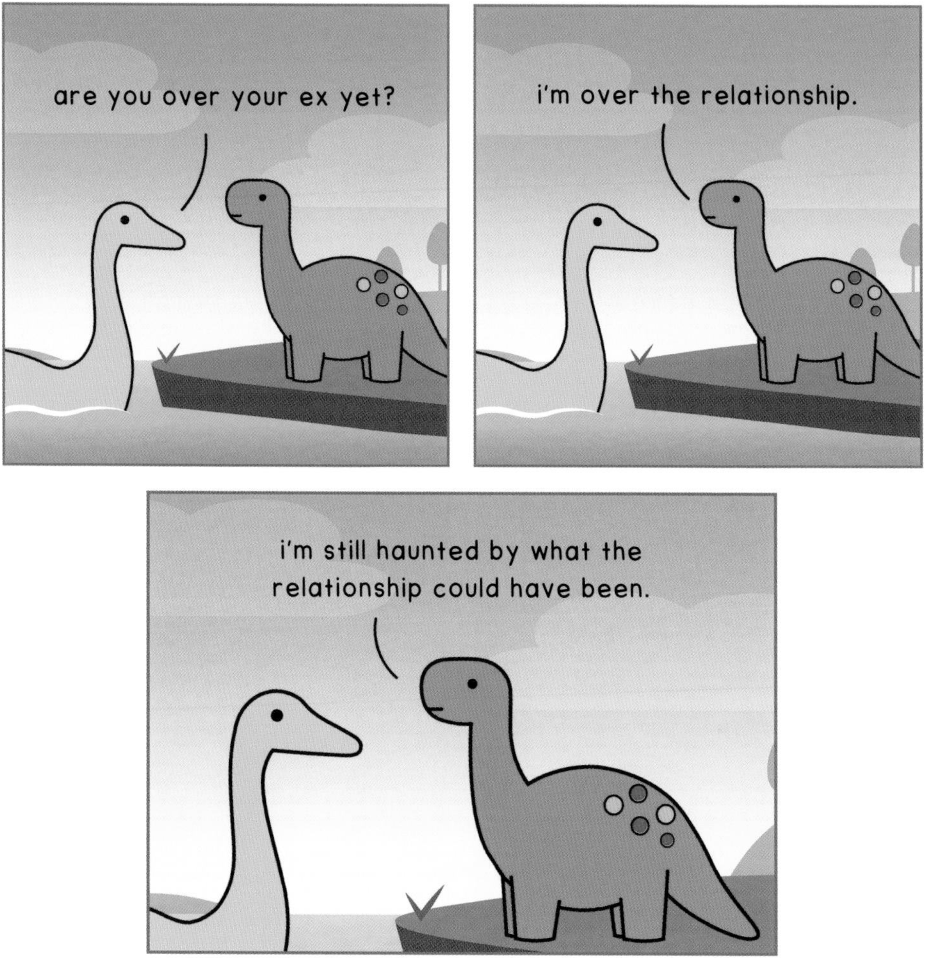
are you over your ex yet?
i'm over the relationship.
i'm still haunted by what the relationship could have been.

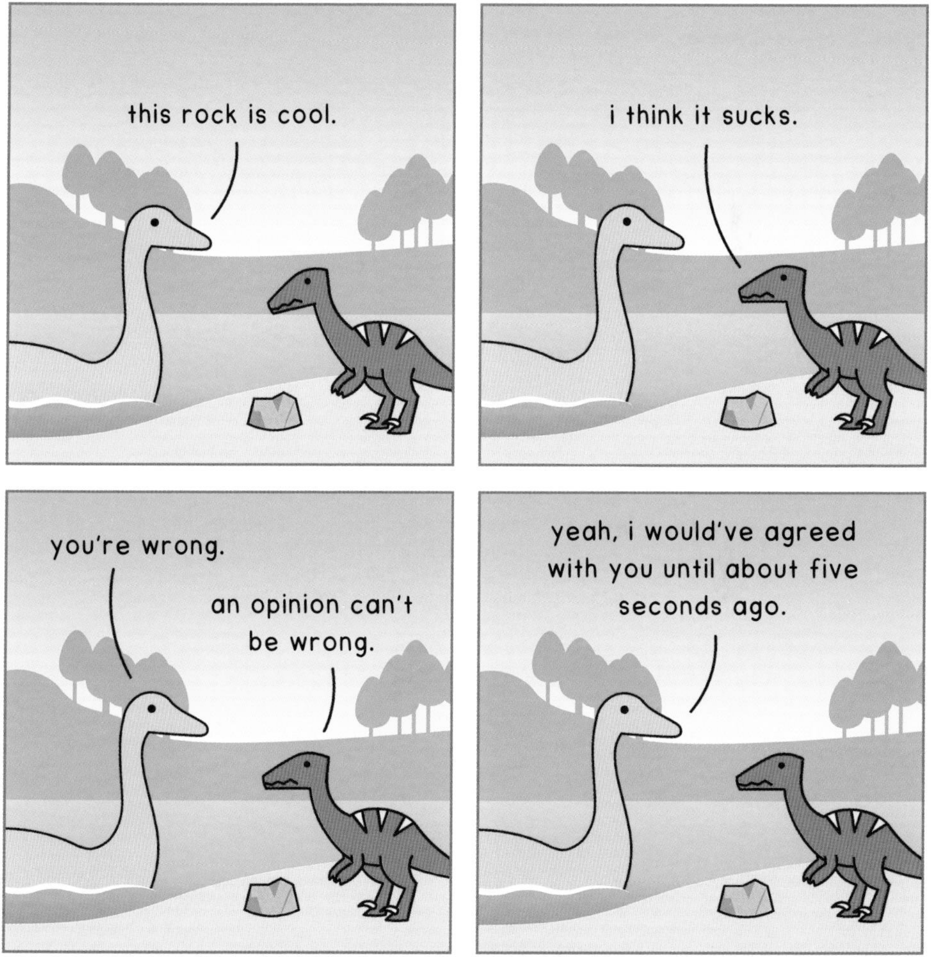
this rock is cool.
i think it sucks.
you're wrong.
an opinion can't be wrong.
yeah, i would've agreed with you until about five seconds ago.

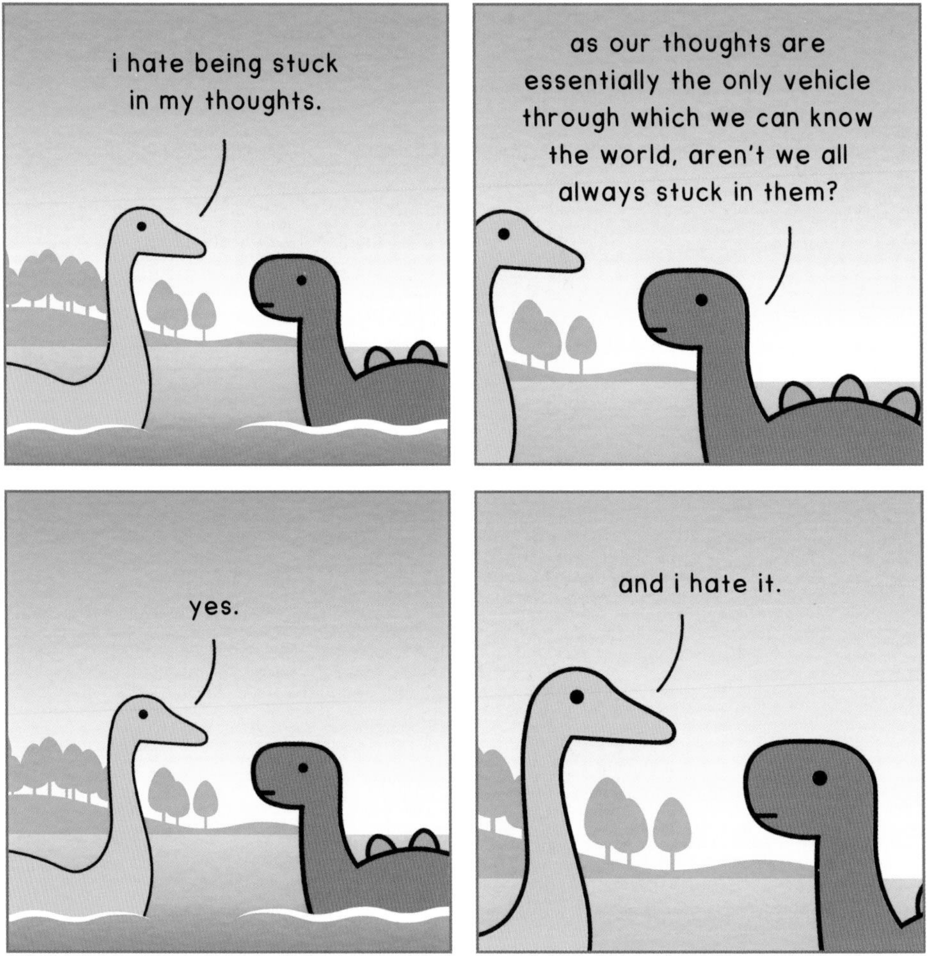
i hate being stuck in my thoughts.
as our thoughts are essentially the only vehicle through which we can know the world, aren't we all always stuck in them?
yes.
and i hate it.

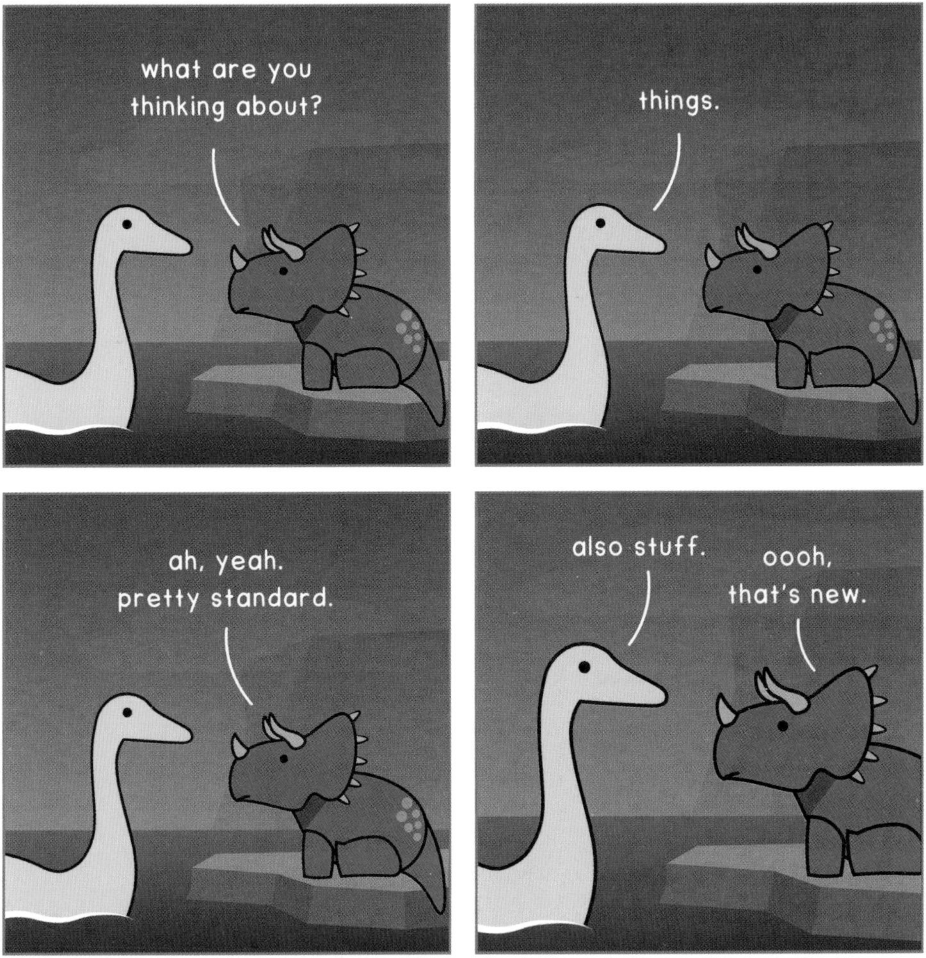
what are you
thinking about?
things.
ah, yeah.
pretty standard.
also stuff.
oooh,
that's new.

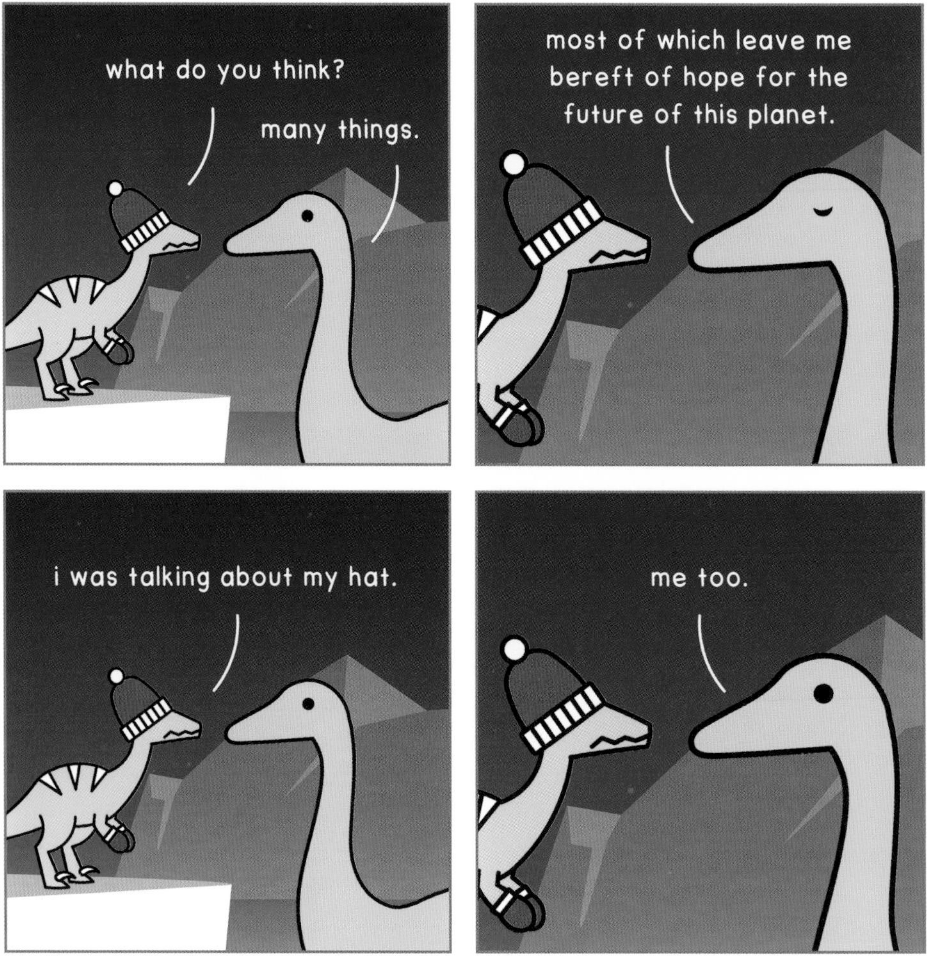
what do you think?
many things.
most of which leave me bereft of hope for the future of this planet.
i was talking about my hat.
me too.

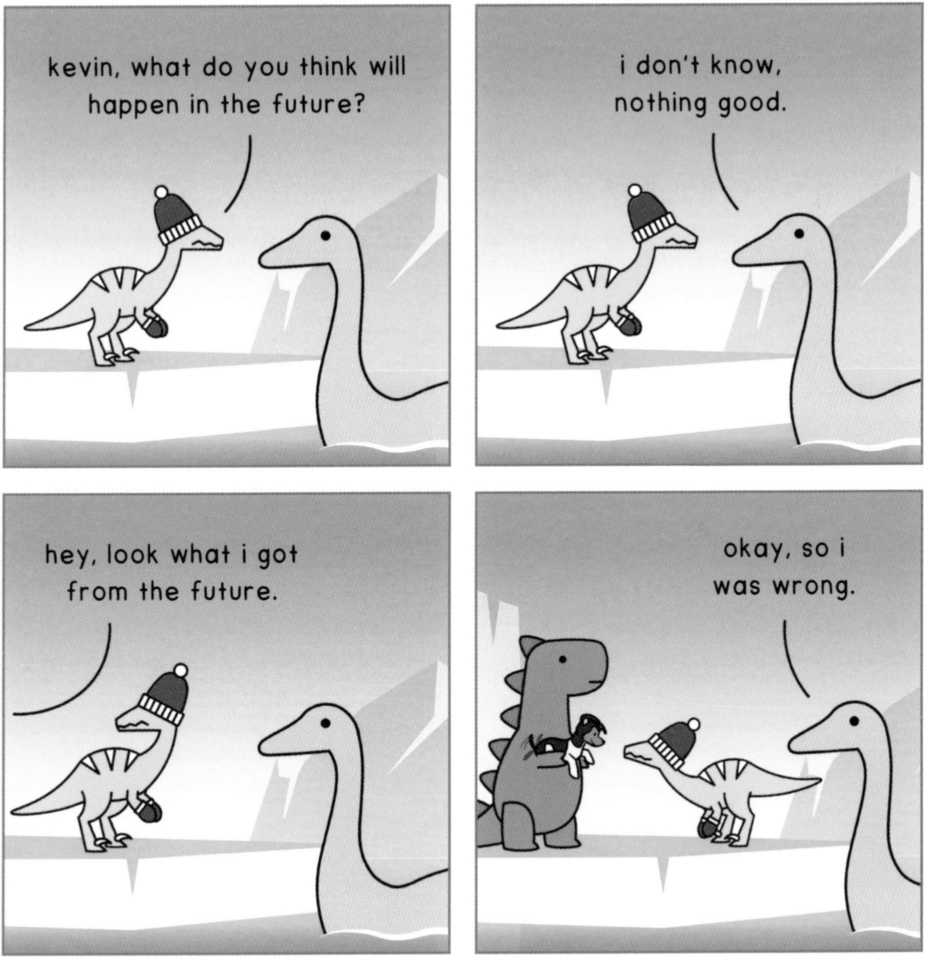
kevin, what do you think will happen in the future?
i don't know, nothing good.
hey, look what i got from the future.
okay, so i was wrong.

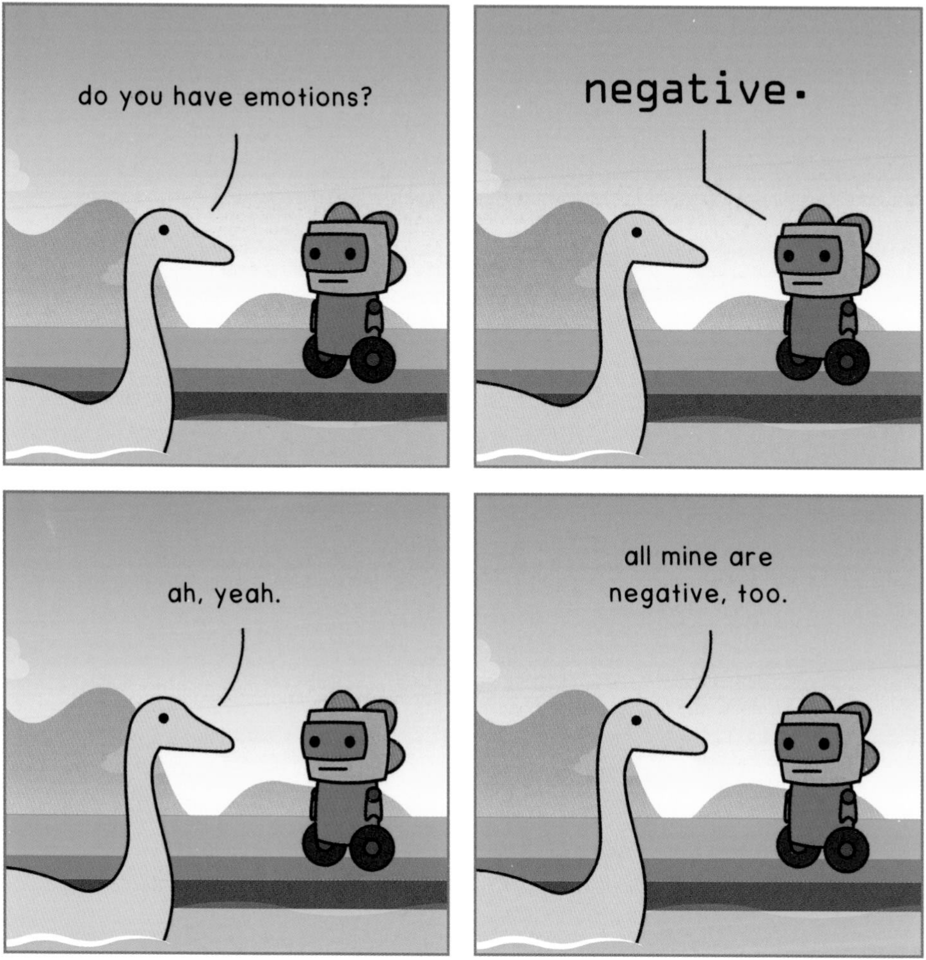
do you have emotions?
negative.
ah, yeah.
all mine are negative, too.

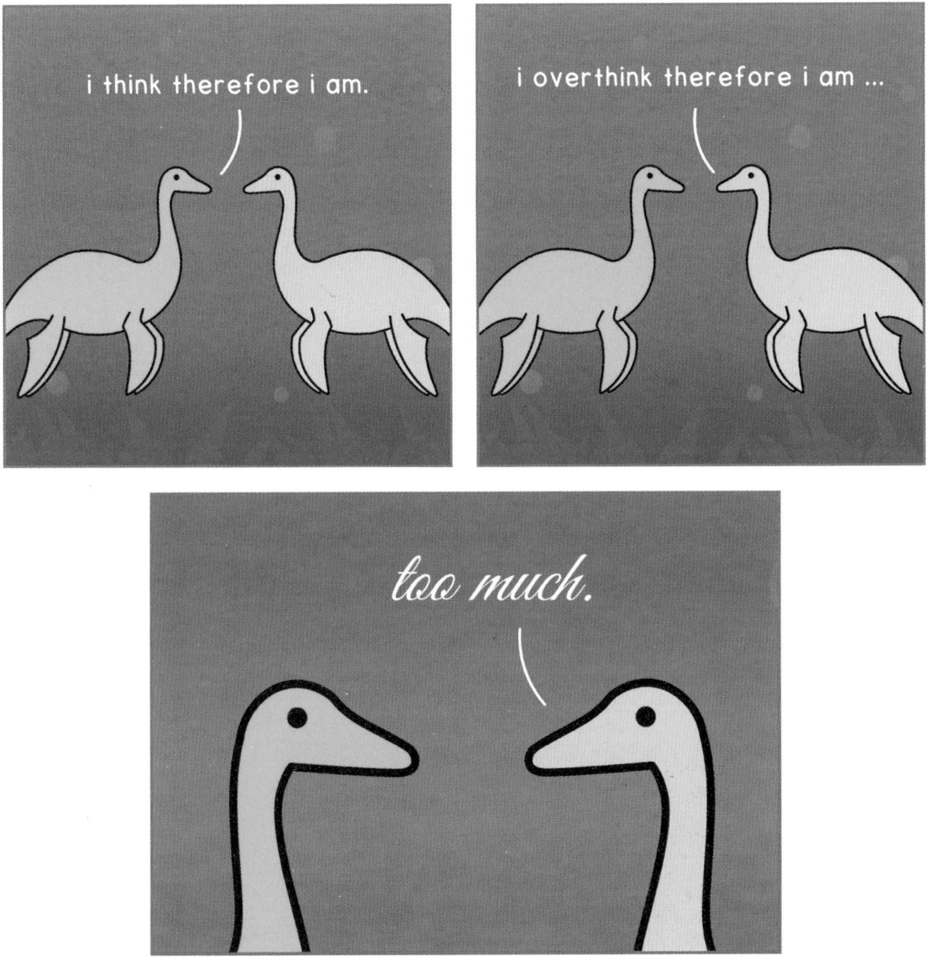
i think therefore i am.
i overthink therefore i am ...
too much.

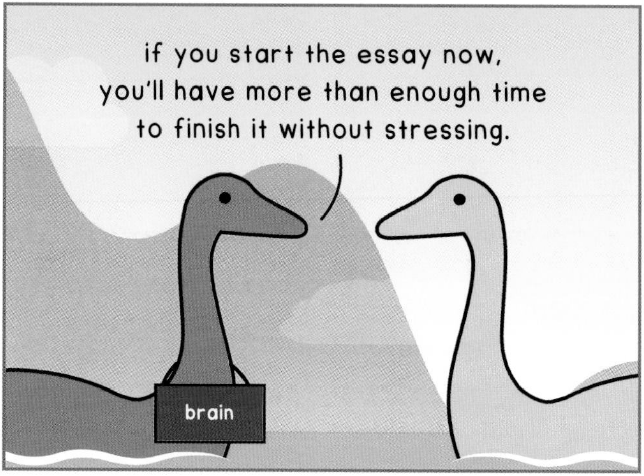
if you start the essay now, you'll have more than enough time to finish it without stressing.
brain

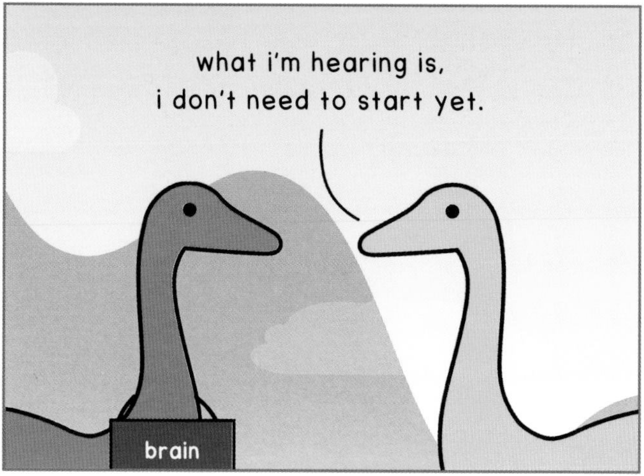
what i'm hearing is, i don't need to start yet.
brain

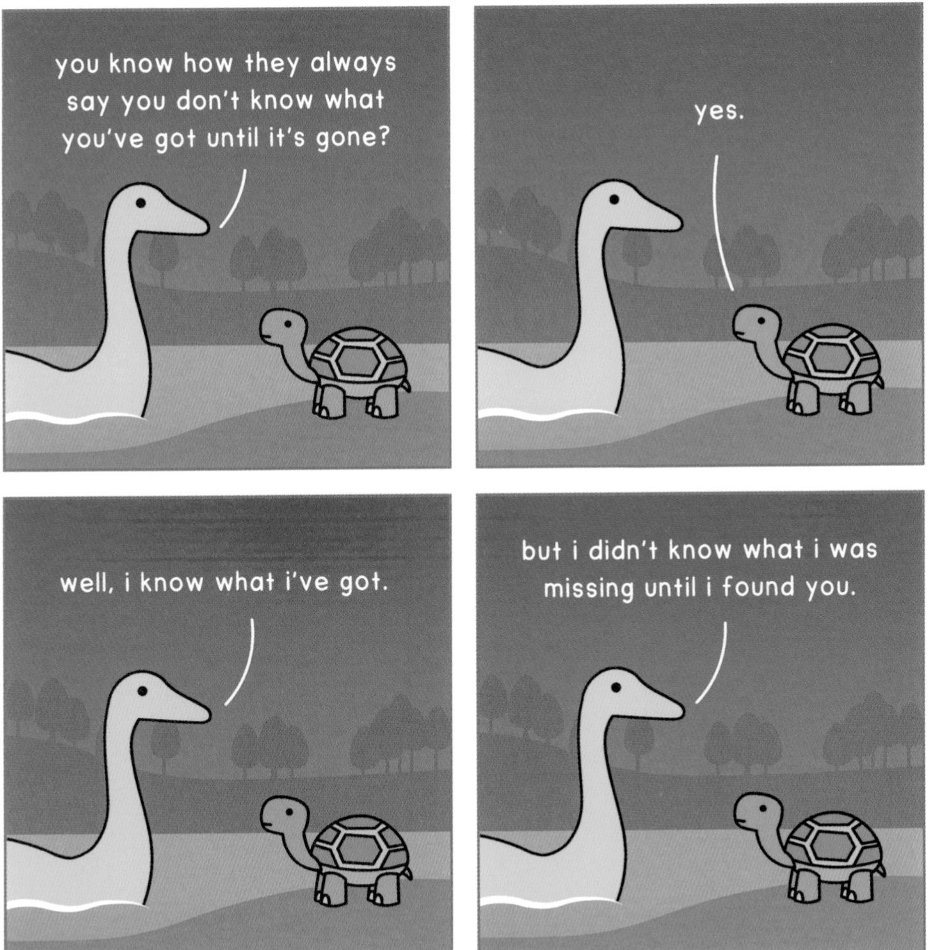
you know how they always say you don't know what you've got until it's gone?
yes.
well, i know what i've got.
but i didn't know what i was missing until i found you.

philosophy
of mind

how do i think?

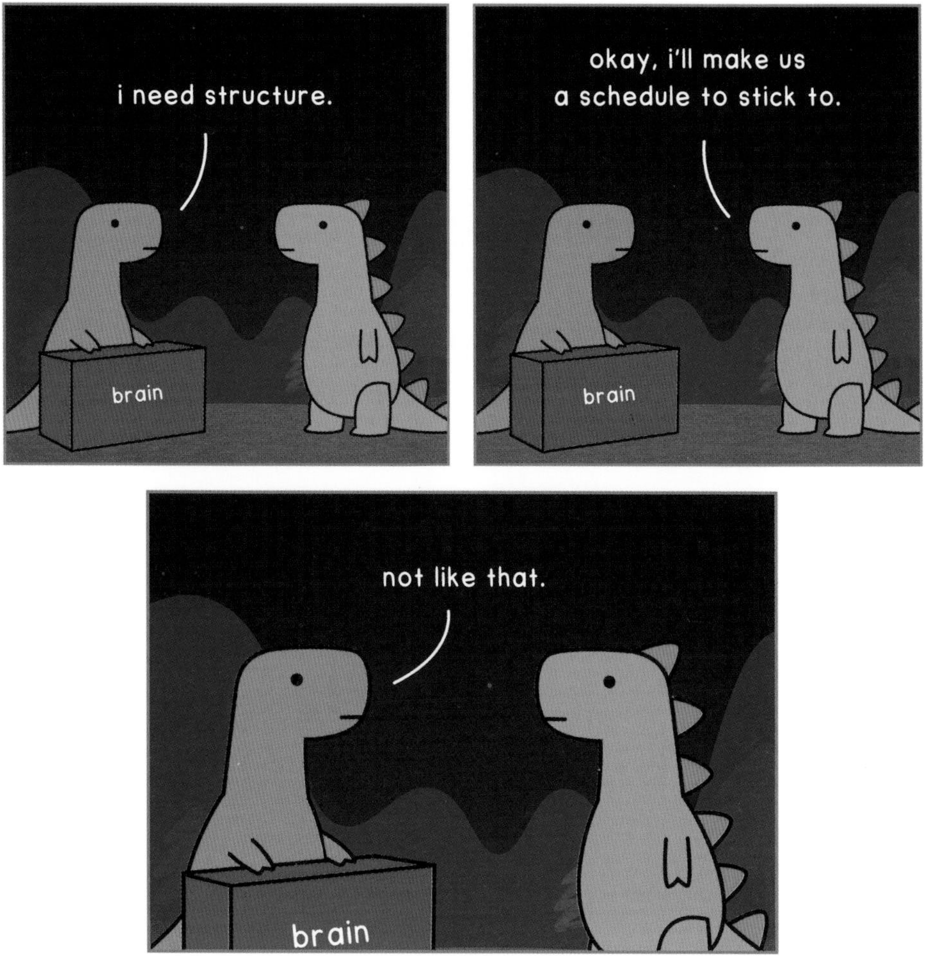
i need structure.
brain
okay, i'll make us
a schedule to stick to.
brain
not like that.
brain

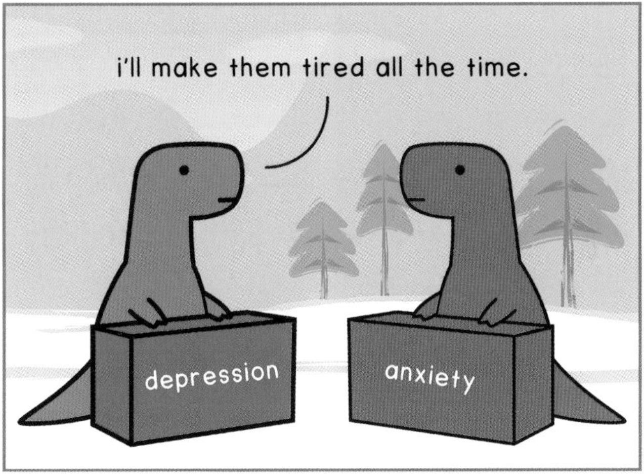
i'll make them tired all the time.
depression
anxiety

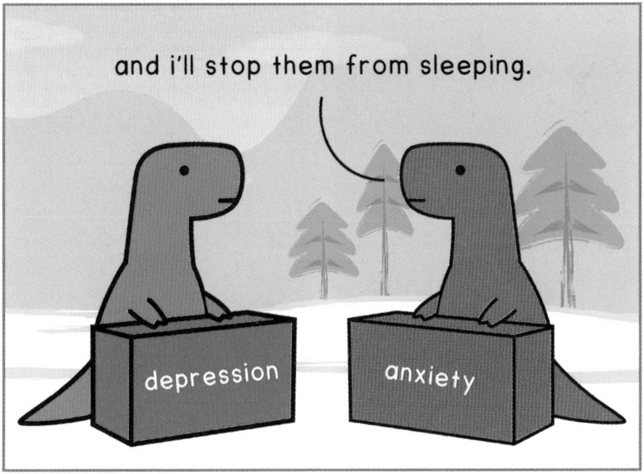
and i'll stop them from sleeping.
depression
anxiety

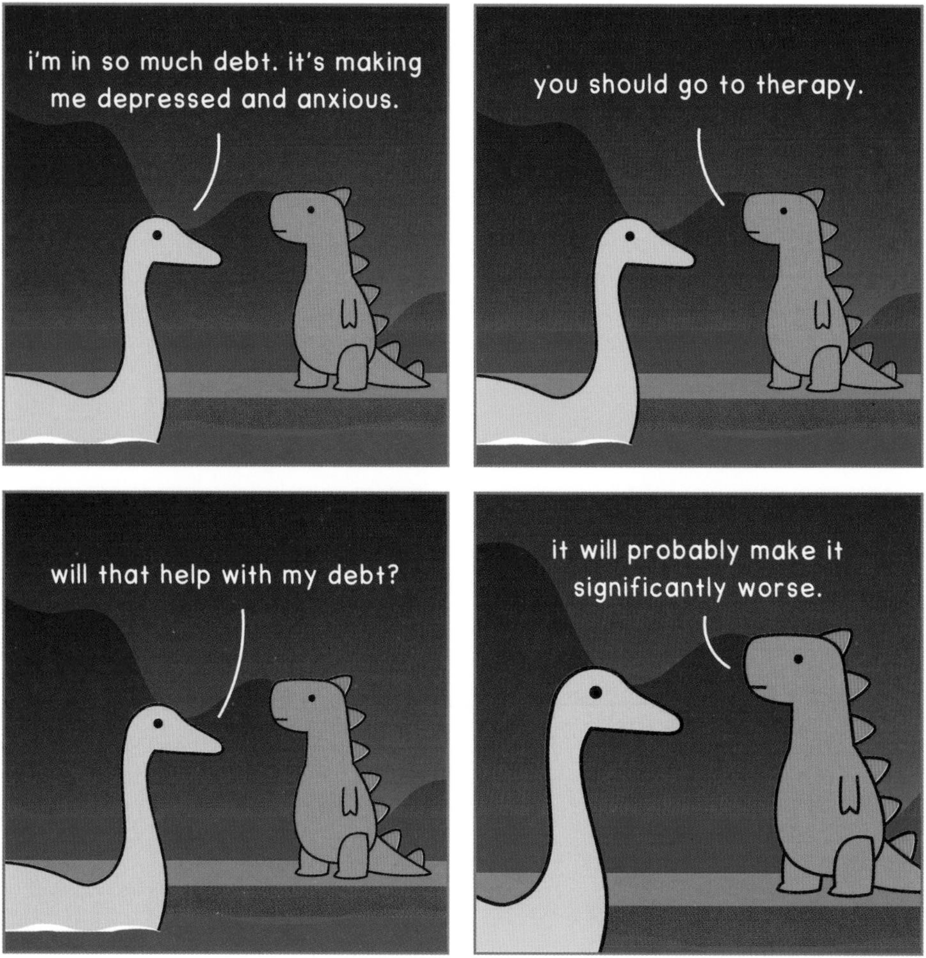
i'm in so much debt. it's making me depressed and anxious.
you should go to therapy.
will that help with my debt?
it will probably make it significantly worse.

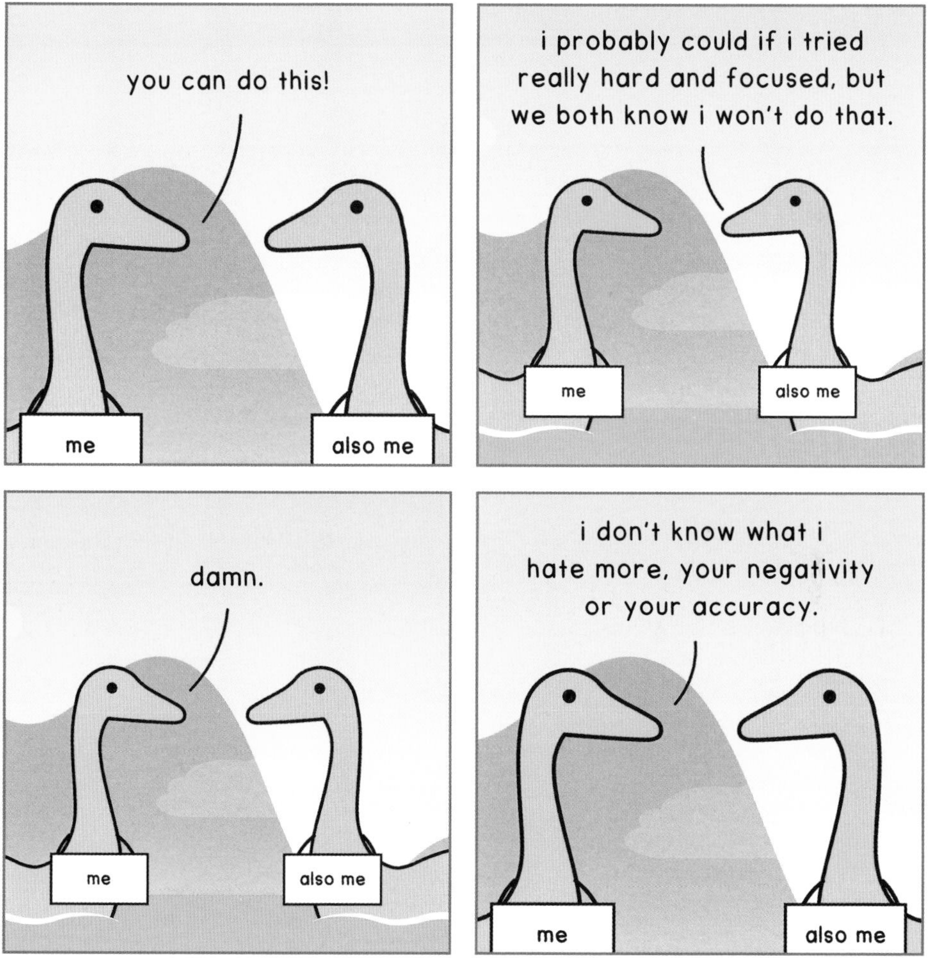
you can do this!
me
also me
i probably could if i tried really hard and focused, but we both know i won't do that.
me
also me
damn.
me
also me
i don't know what i hate more, your negativity or your accuracy.
me
also me

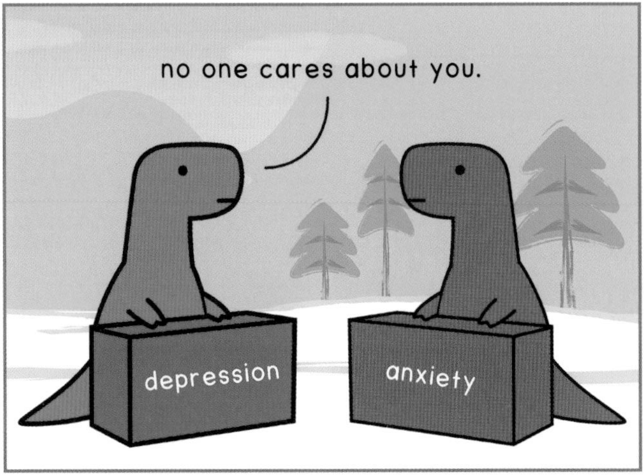
no one cares about you.
depression
anxiety

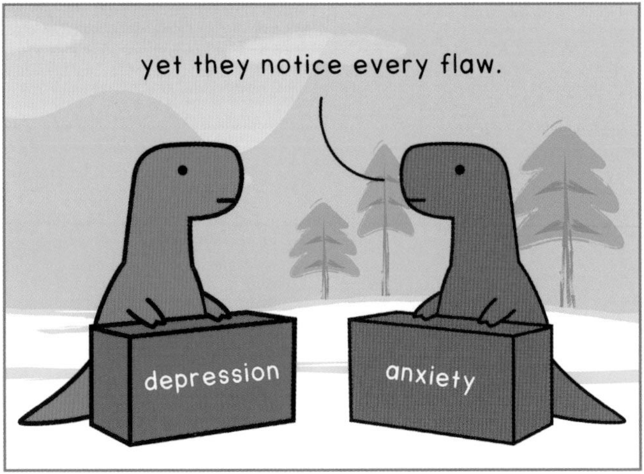
yet they notice every flaw.
depression
anxiety

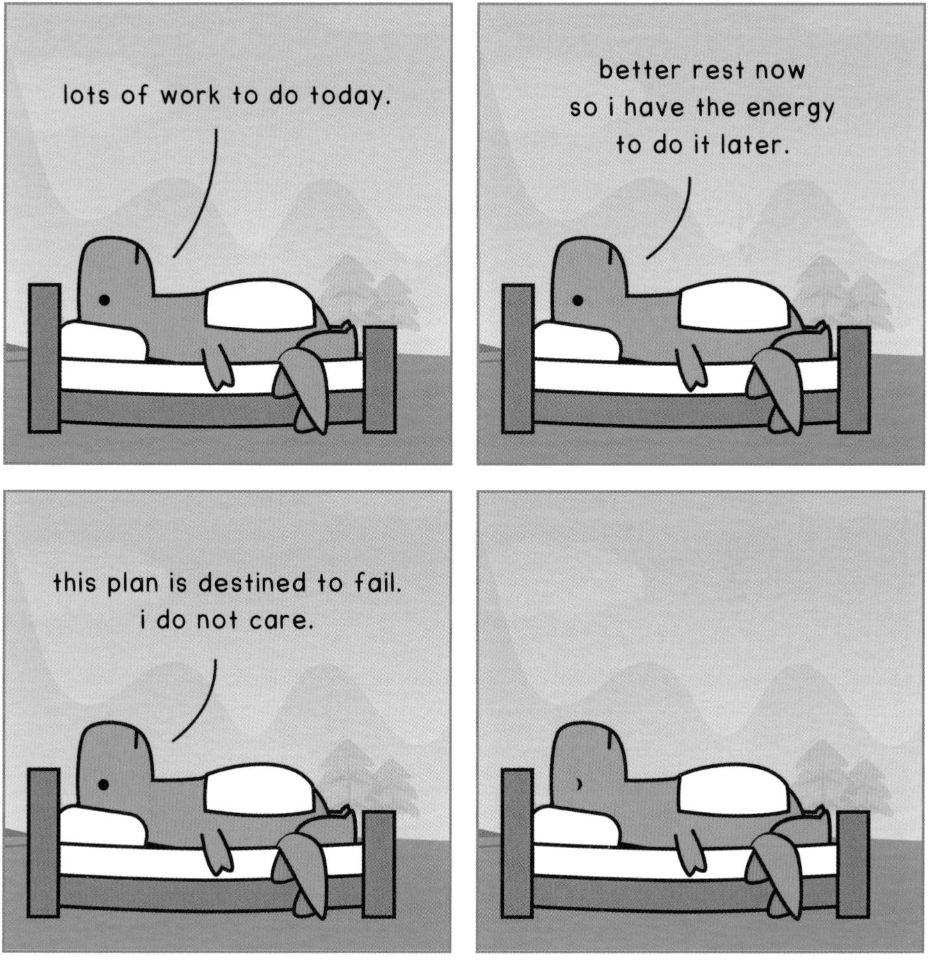
lots of work to do today.
better rest now so i have the energy to do it later.
this plan is destined to fail. i do not care.

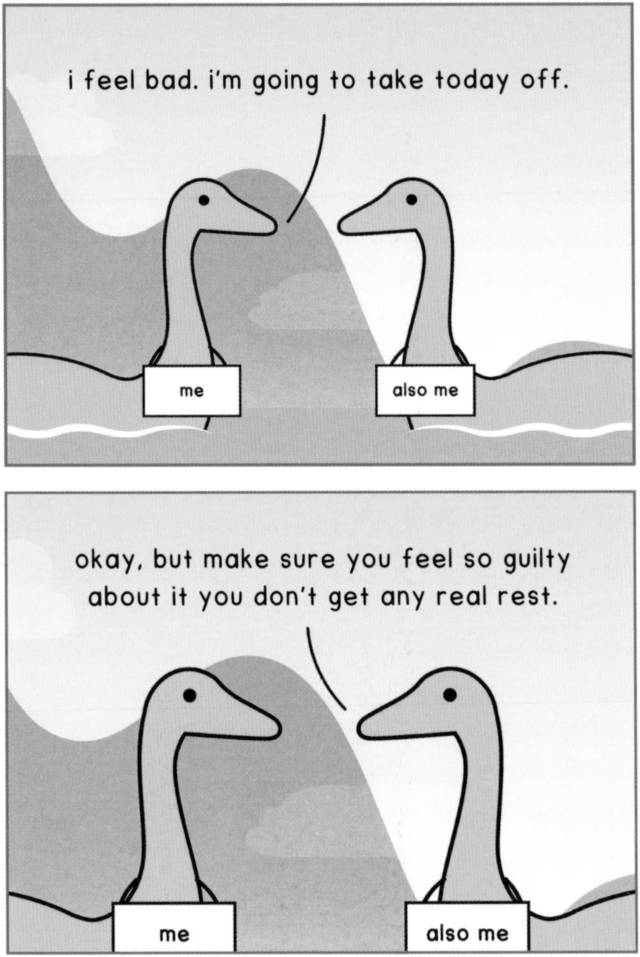
i feel bad. i'm going to take today off.
me
also me
okay, but make sure you feel so guilty about it you don't get any real rest.
me
also me

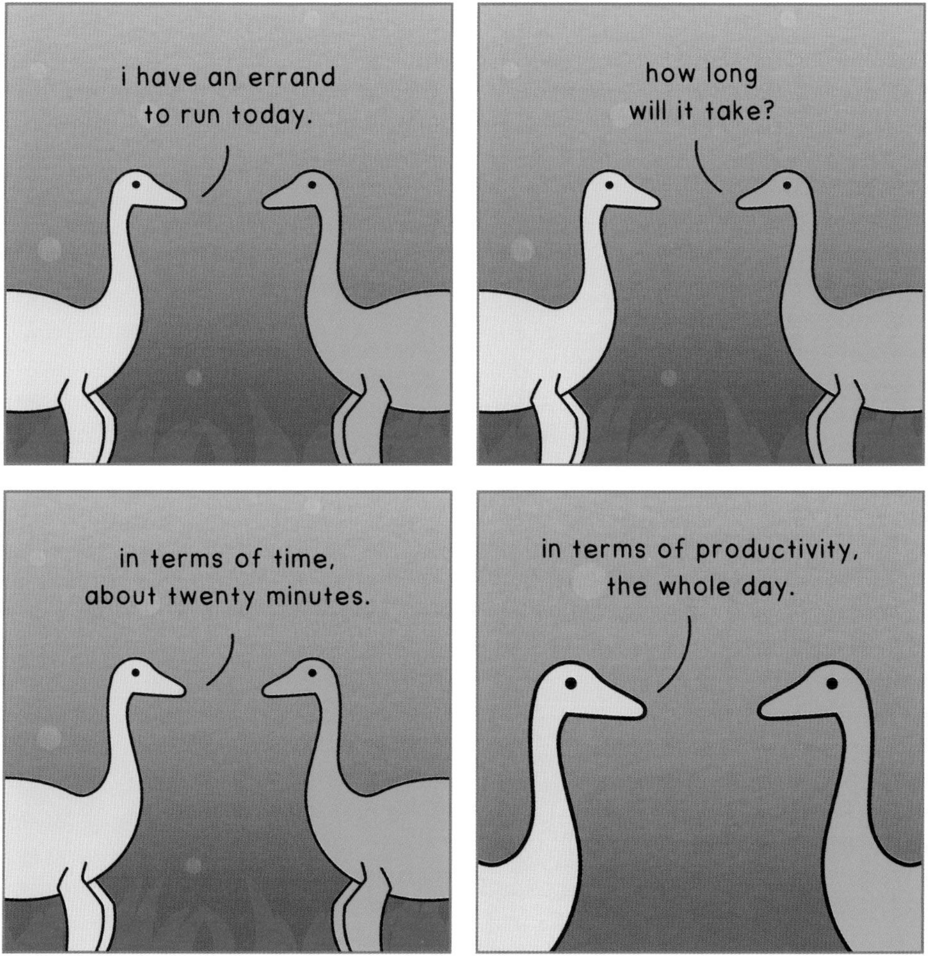
i have an errand to run today.
how long will it take?
in terms of time, about twenty minutes.
in terms of productivity, the whole day.

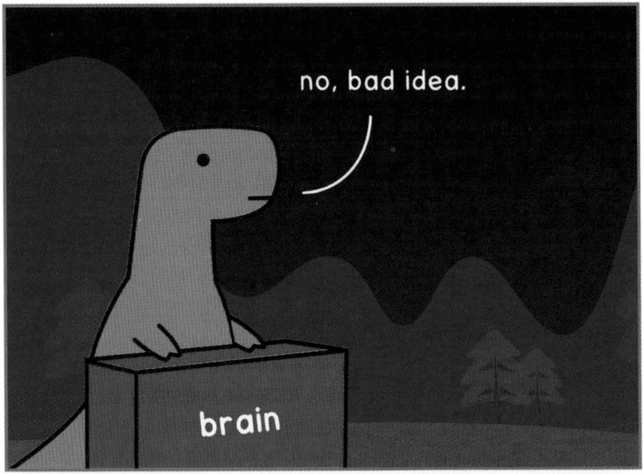
no, bad idea.
brain

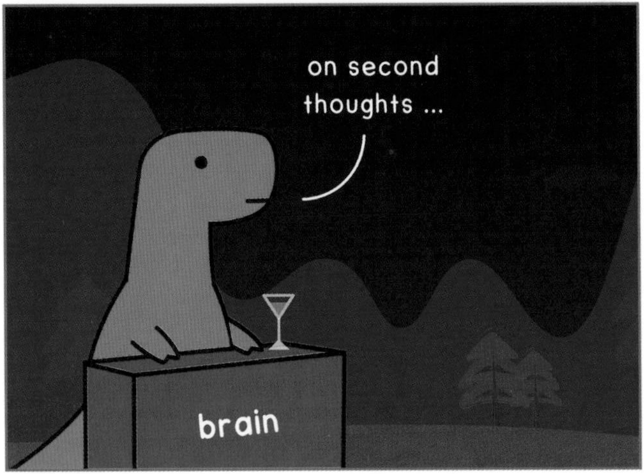
on second thoughts ...
brain

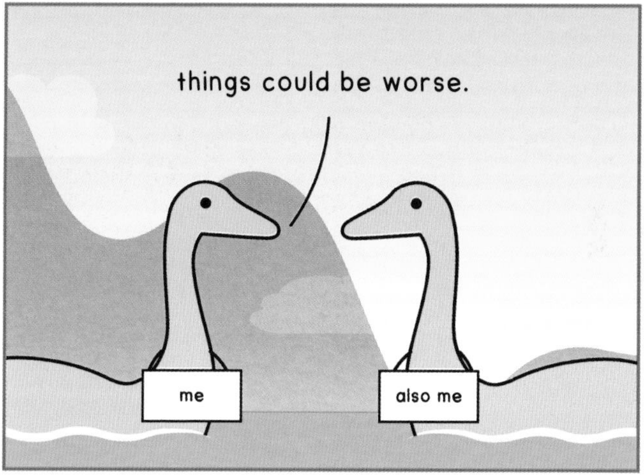
things could be worse.
me
also me

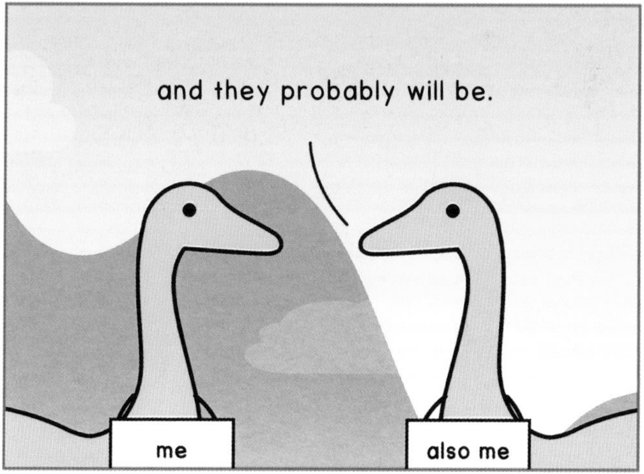
and they probably will be.
me
also me

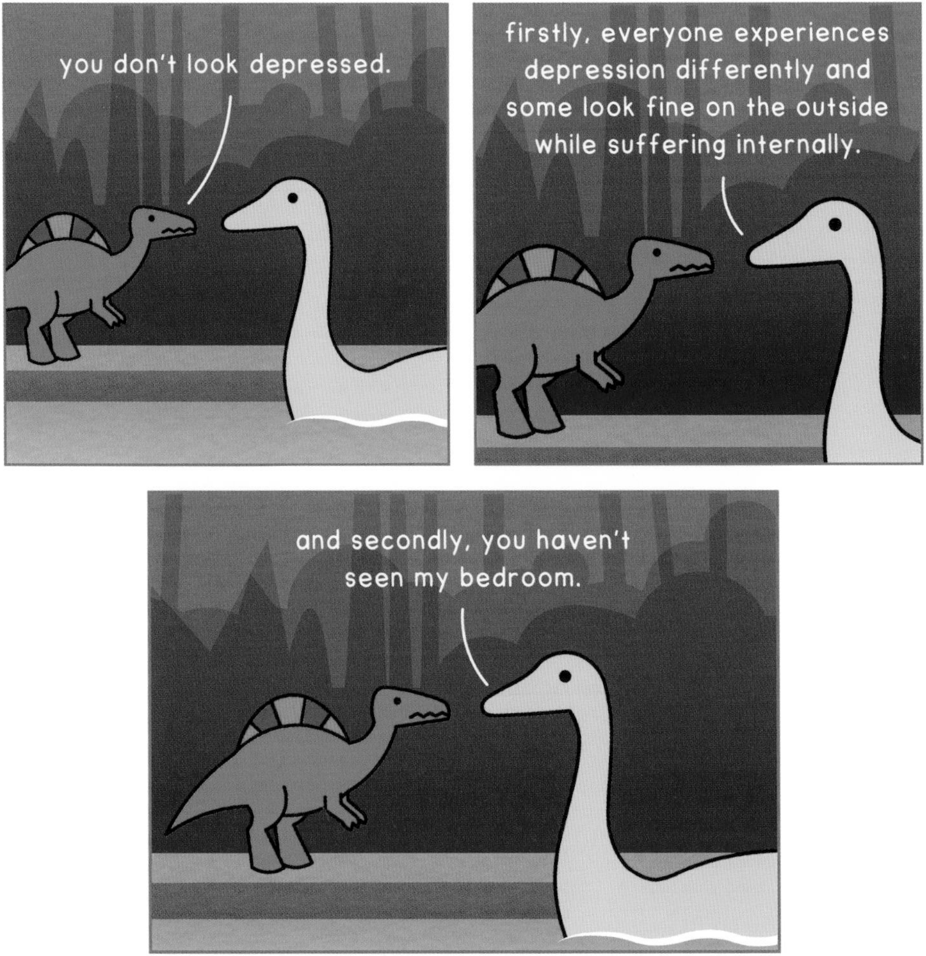
you don't look depressed.
firstly, everyone experiences depression differently and some look fine on the outside while suffering internally.
and secondly, you haven't seen my bedroom.

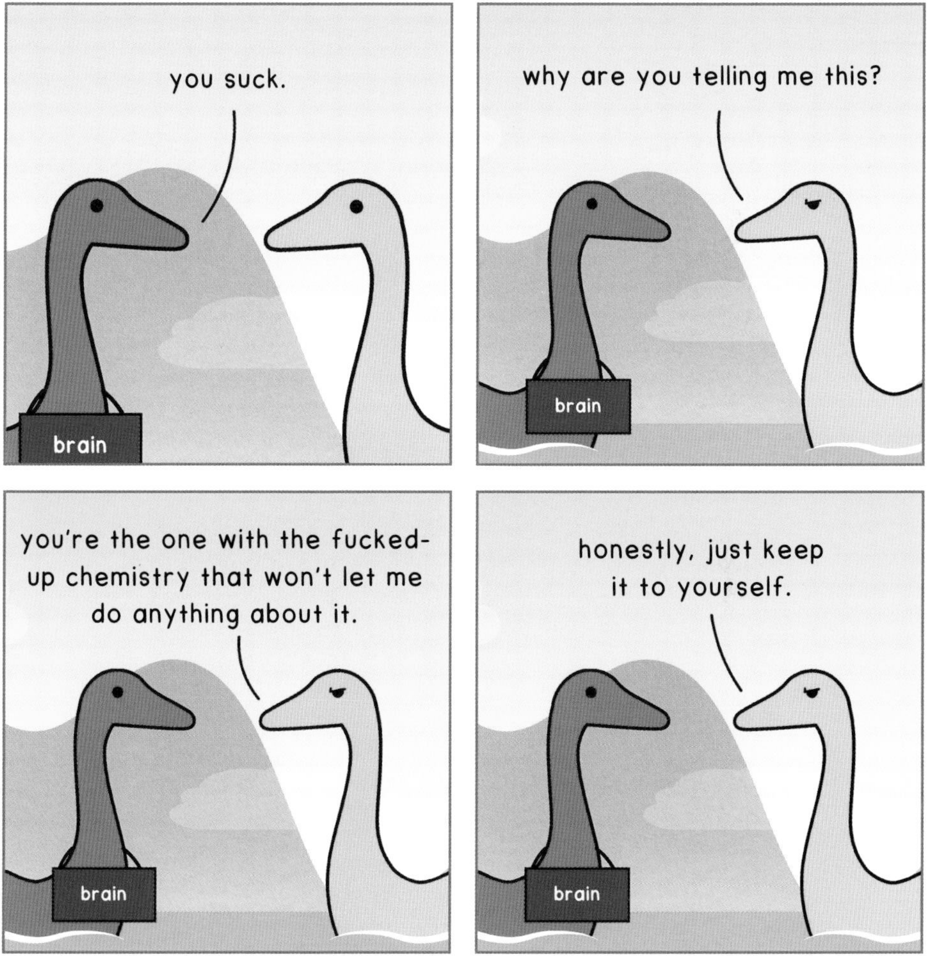
you suck.
brain
why are you telling me this?
brain
you're the one with the fucked-up chemistry that won't let me do anything about it.
brain
honestly, just keep it to yourself.
brain

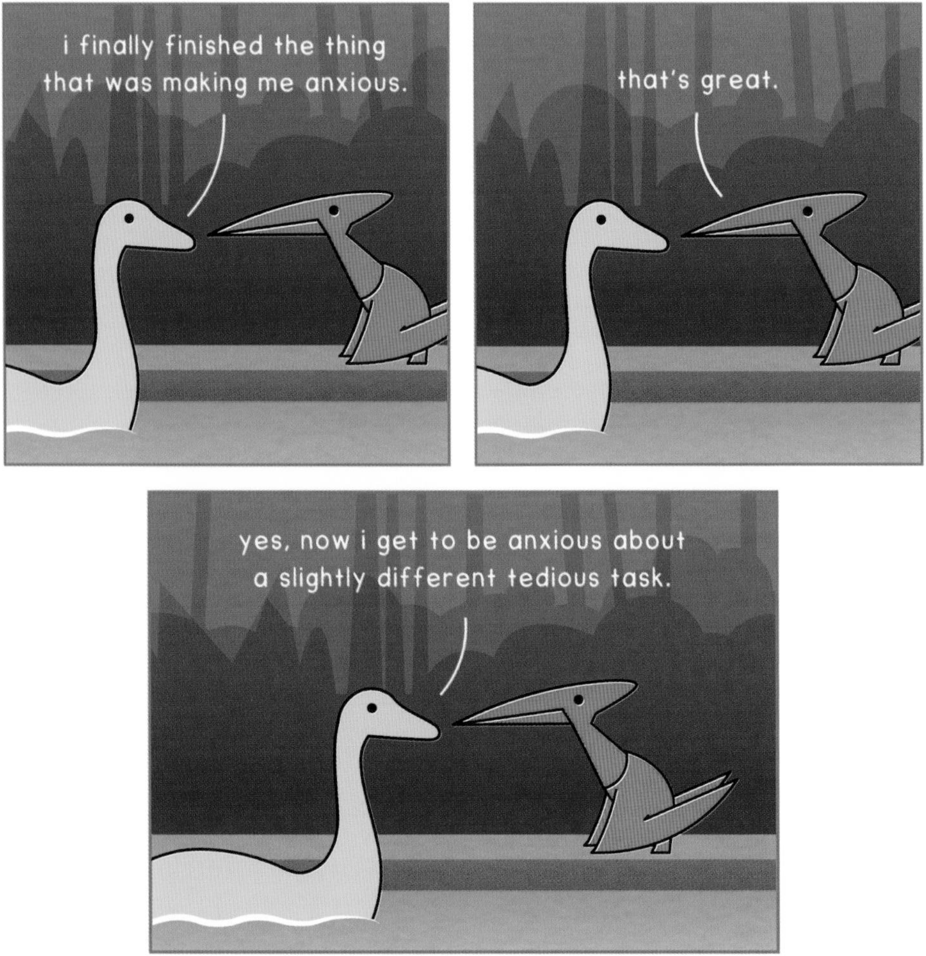
i finally finished the thing that was making me anxious.
that's great.
yes, now i get to be anxious about a slightly different tedious task.

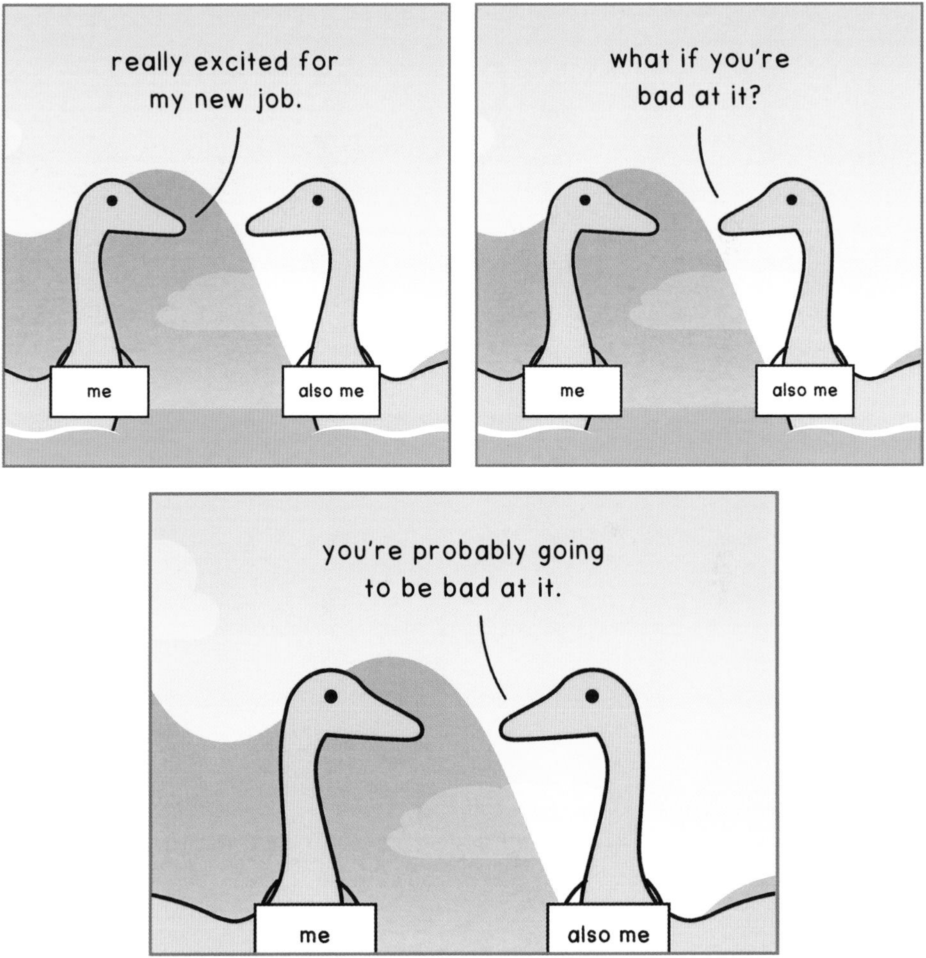
really excited for my new job.
me
also me
what if you're bad at it?
me
also me
you're probably going to be bad at it.
me
also me

what's the worst that could happen?
me
also me
i'm glad you asked.
me
also me
i have so many ideas.
me
also me

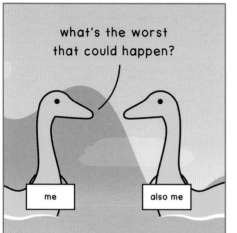

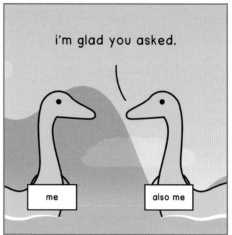

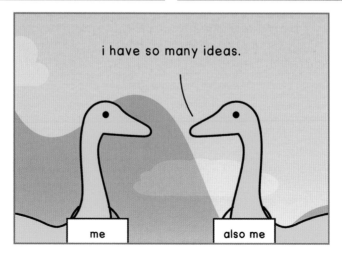

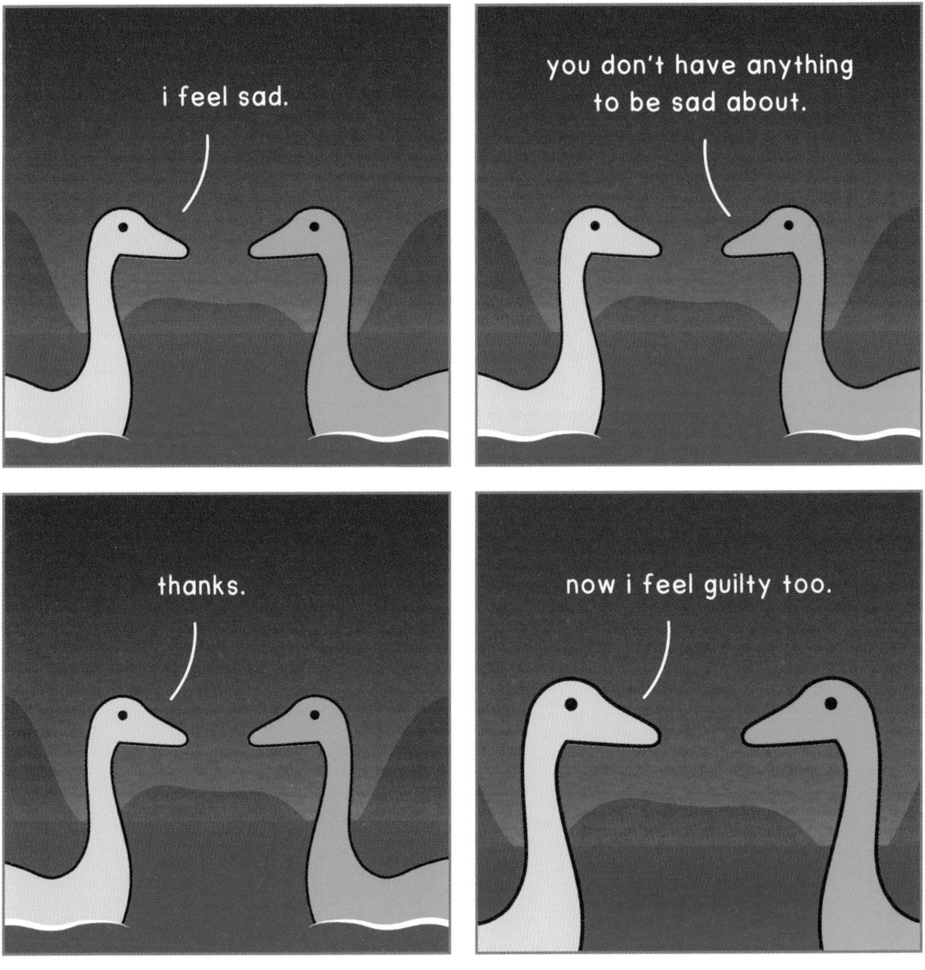
i feel sad.
you don't have anything to be sad about.
thanks.
now i feel guilty too.

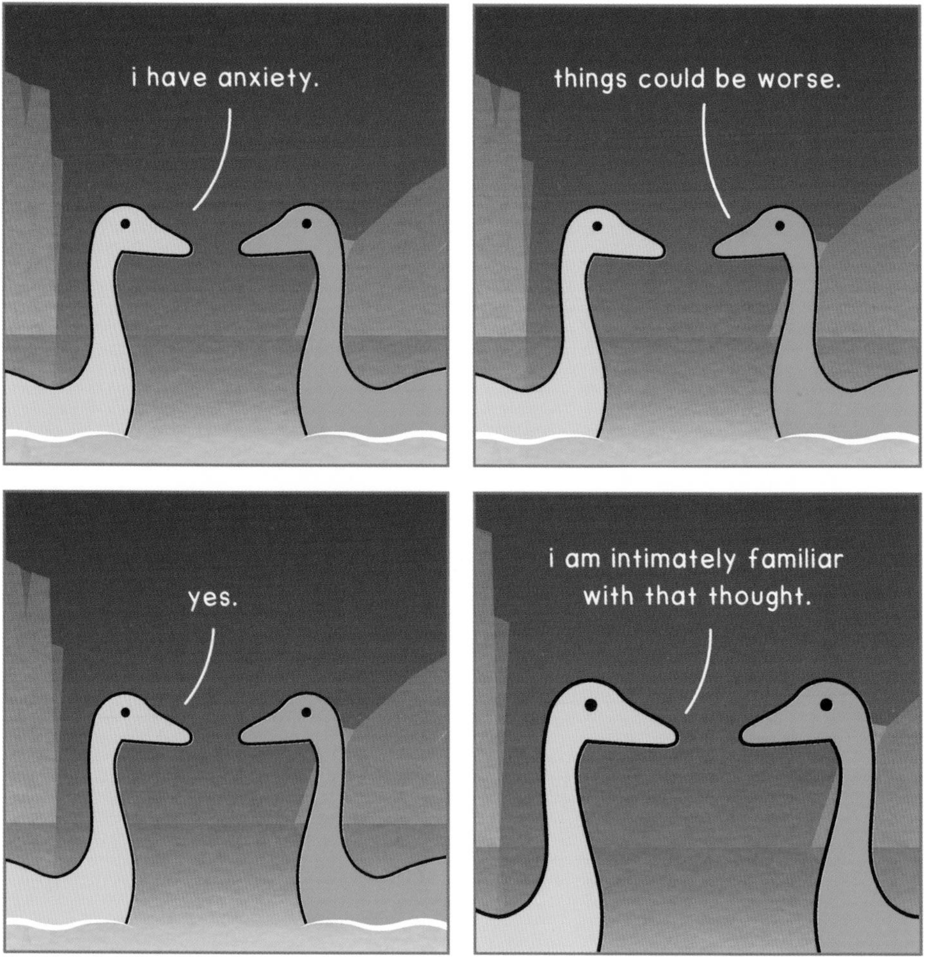
i have anxiety.
things could be worse.
yes.
i am intimately familiar with that thought.

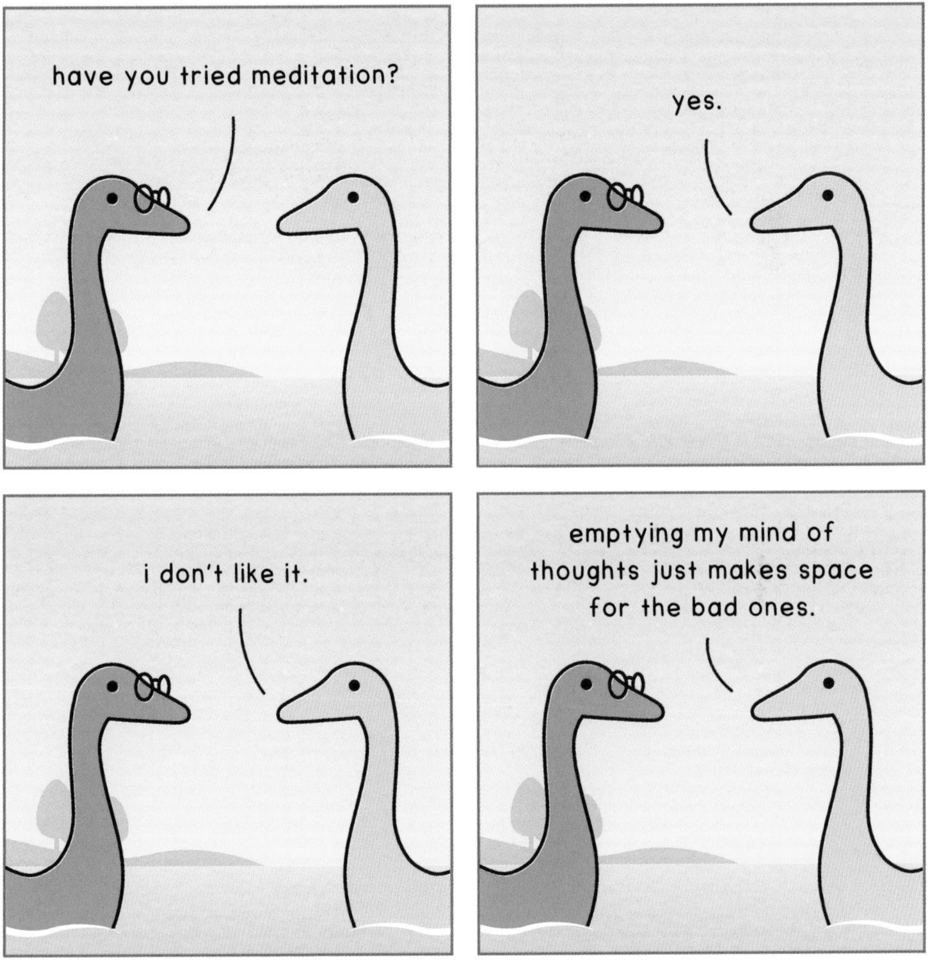
have you tried meditation?
yes.
i don't like it.
emptying my mind of thoughts just makes space for the bad ones.

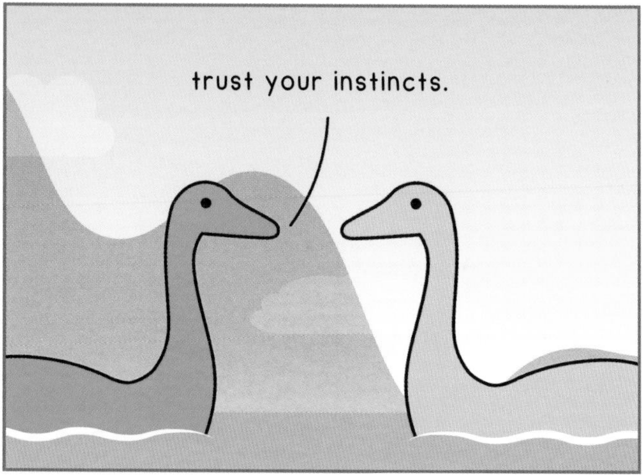
trust your instincts.

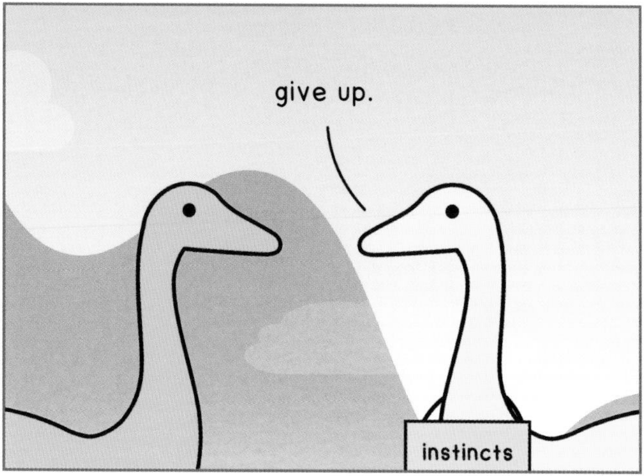
give up.
instincts

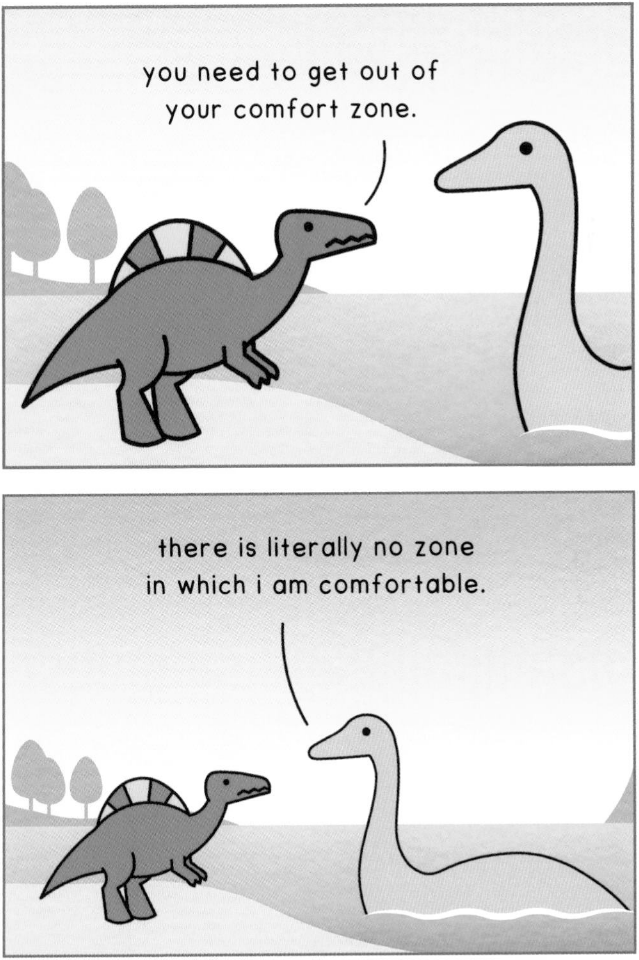
you need to get out of your comfort zone.
there is literally no zone in which i am comfortable.

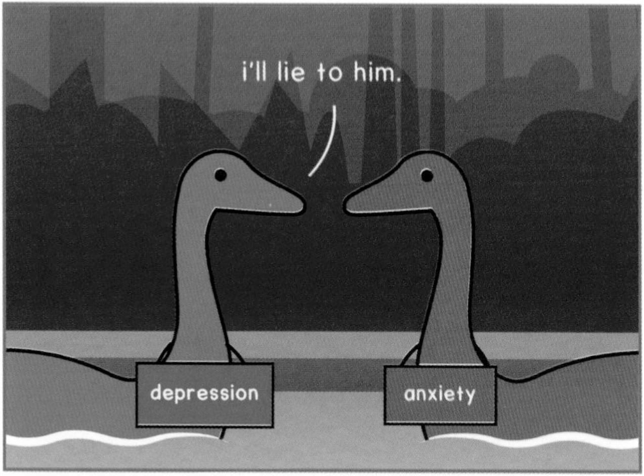
i'll lie to him.
depression
anxiety

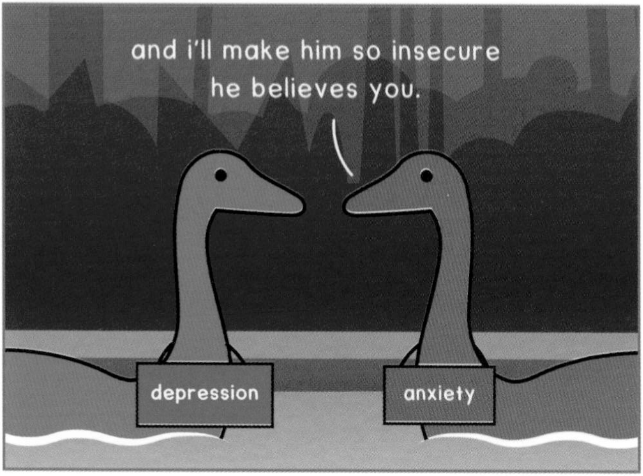
and i'll make him so insecure he believes you.
depression
anxiety

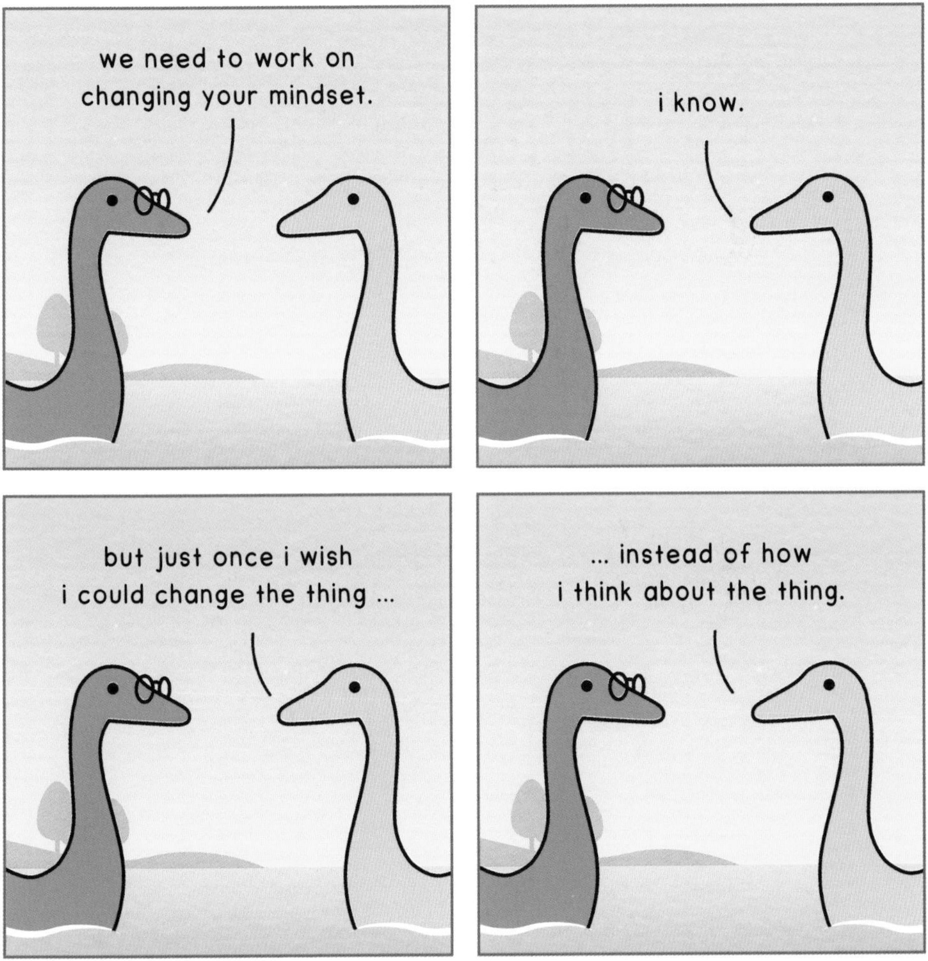
we need to work on
changing your mindset.
i know.
but just once i wish
i could change the thing ...
... instead of how
i think about the thing.

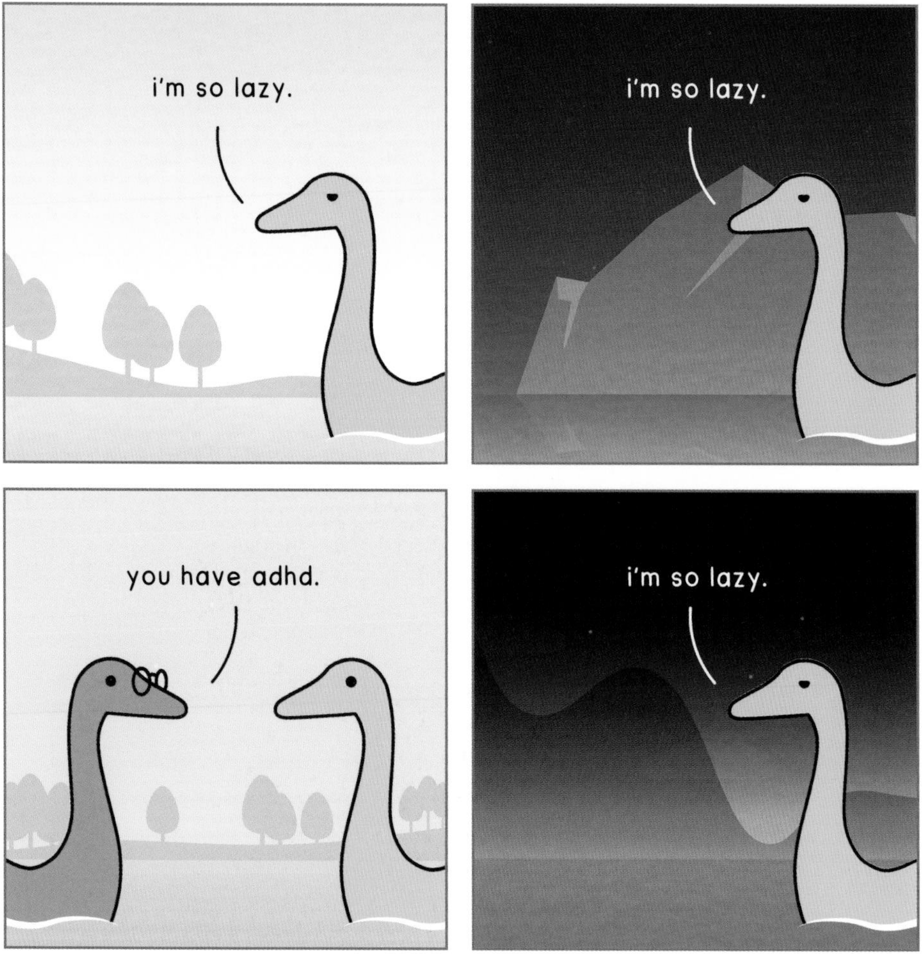

i'm so lazy.
i'm so lazy.
you have adhd.
i'm so lazy.

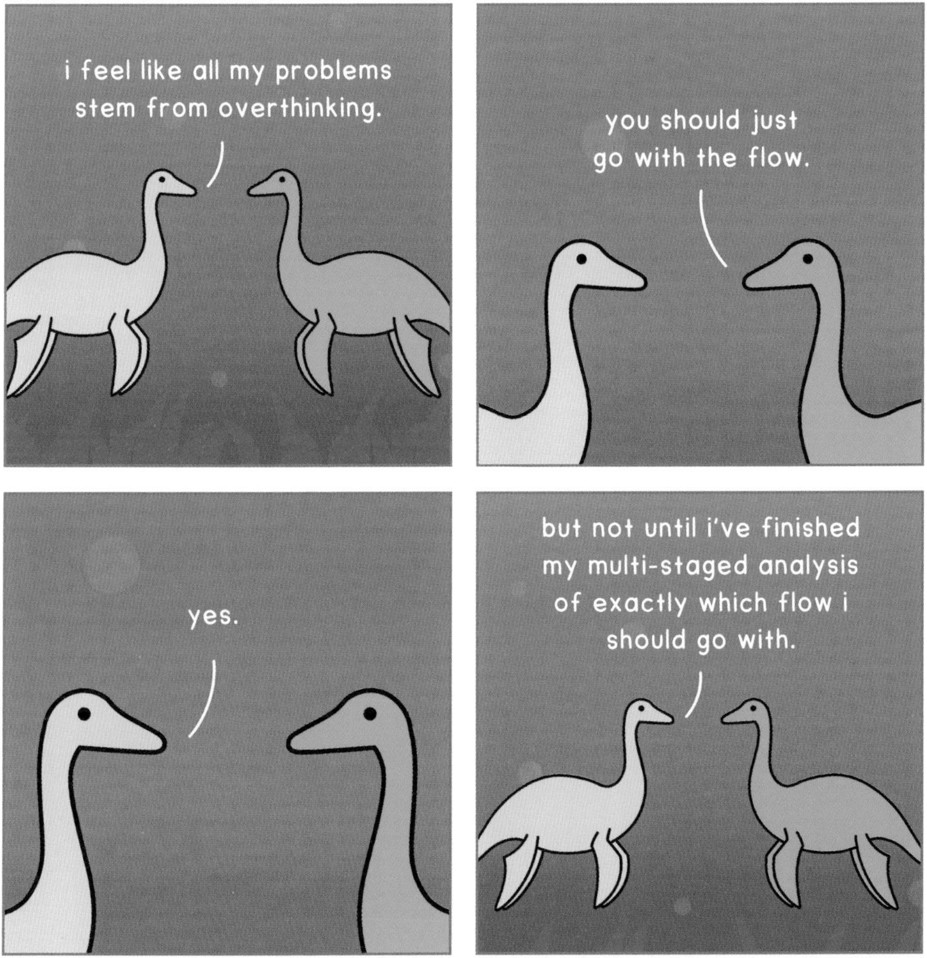
i feel like all my problems stem from overthinking.
you should just go with the flow.
yes.
but not until i've finished my multi-staged analysis of exactly which flow i should go with.

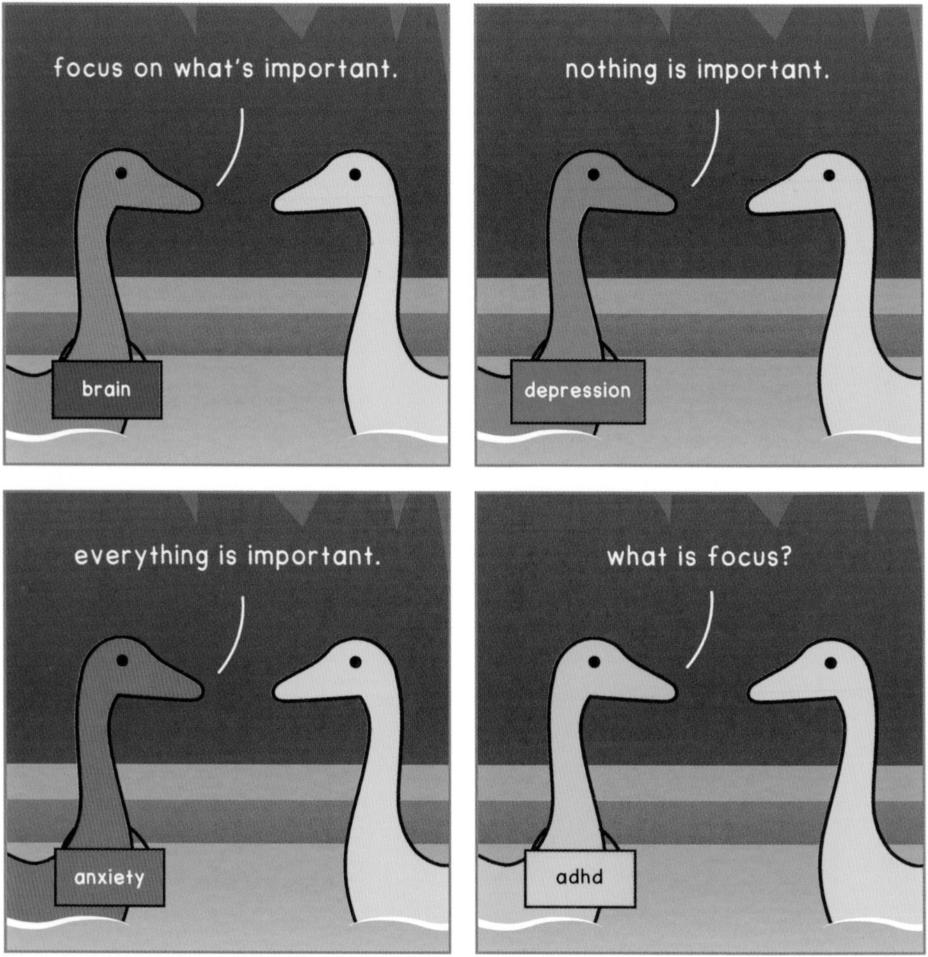
focus on what's important.
brain
nothing is important.
depression
everything is important.
anxiety
what is focus?
adhd

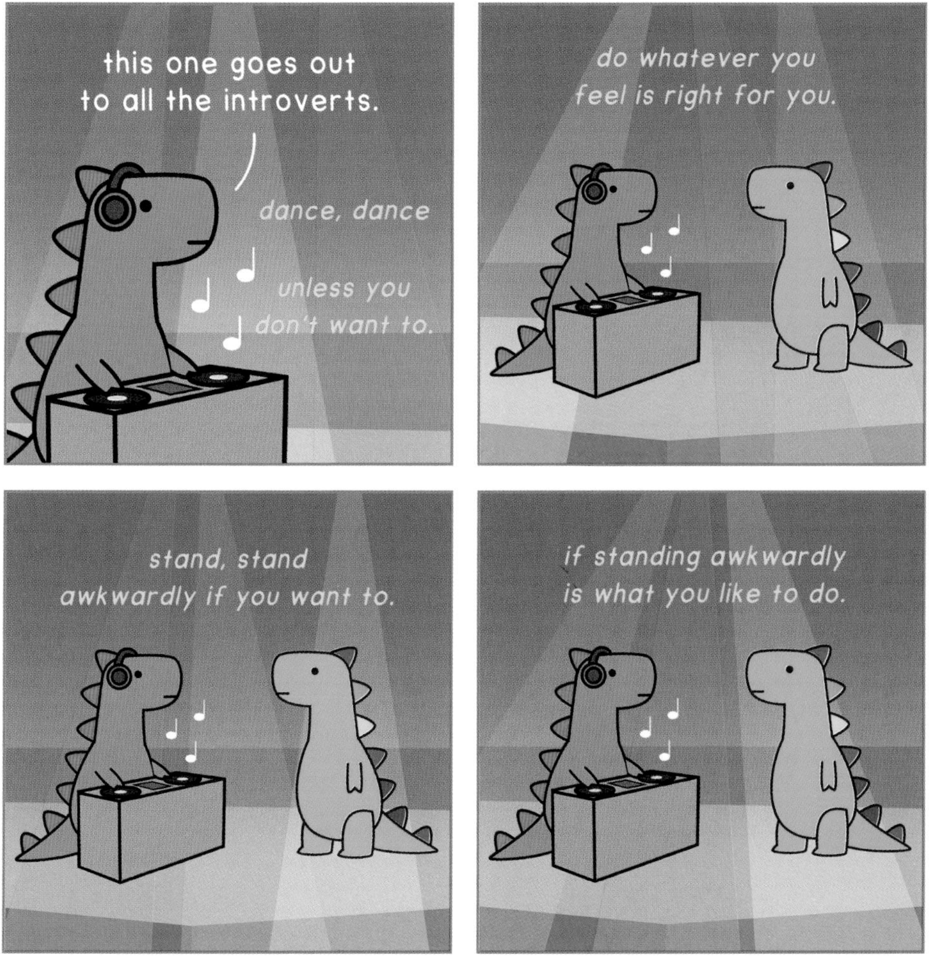

this one goes out
to all the introverts.
dance, dance
unless you
don't want to.
do whatever you
feel is right for you.
stand, stand
awkwardly if you want to.
if standing awkwardly
is what you like to do.

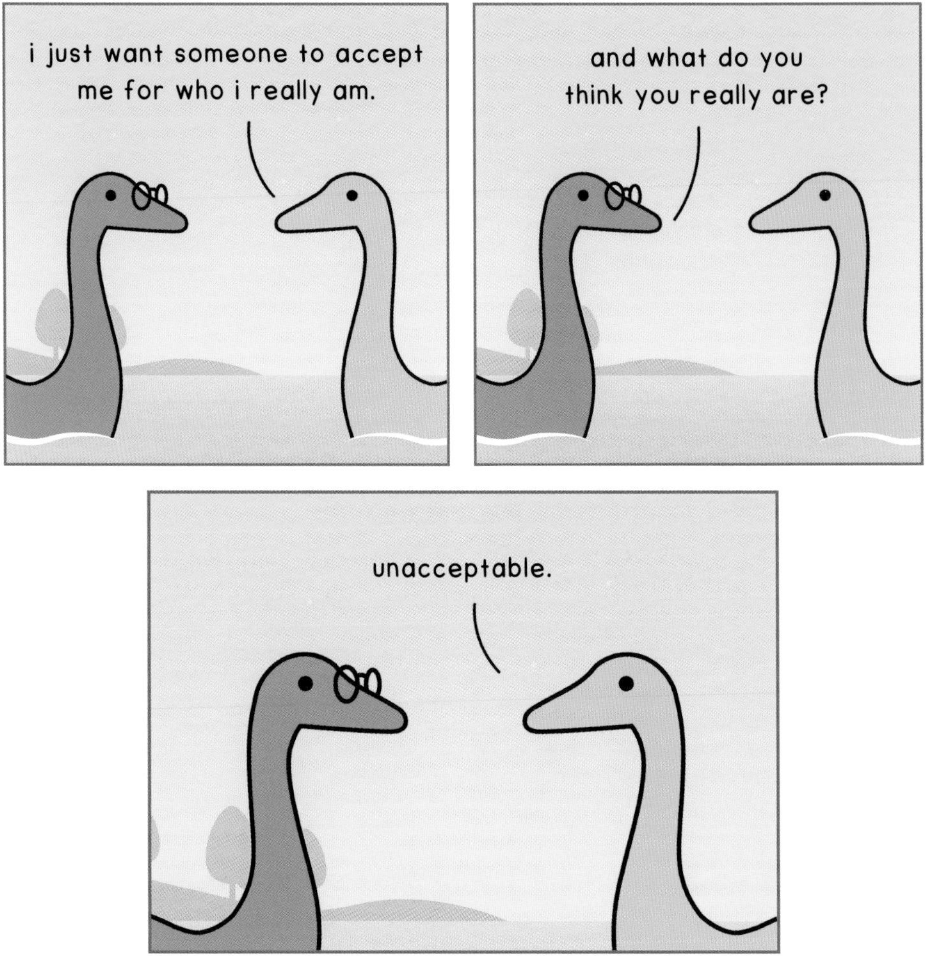
i just want someone to accept me for who i really am.
and what do you think you really are?
unacceptable.

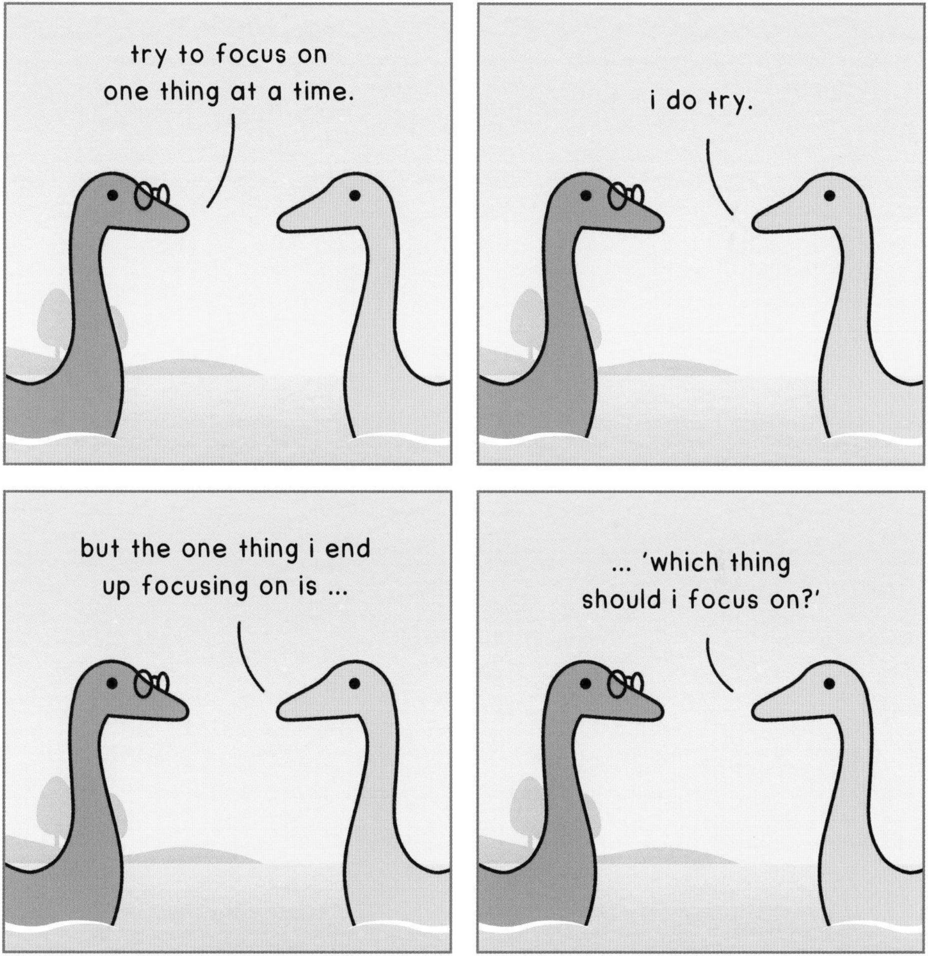
try to focus on one thing at a time.
i do try.
but the one thing i end up focusing on is ...
... 'which thing should i focus on?'

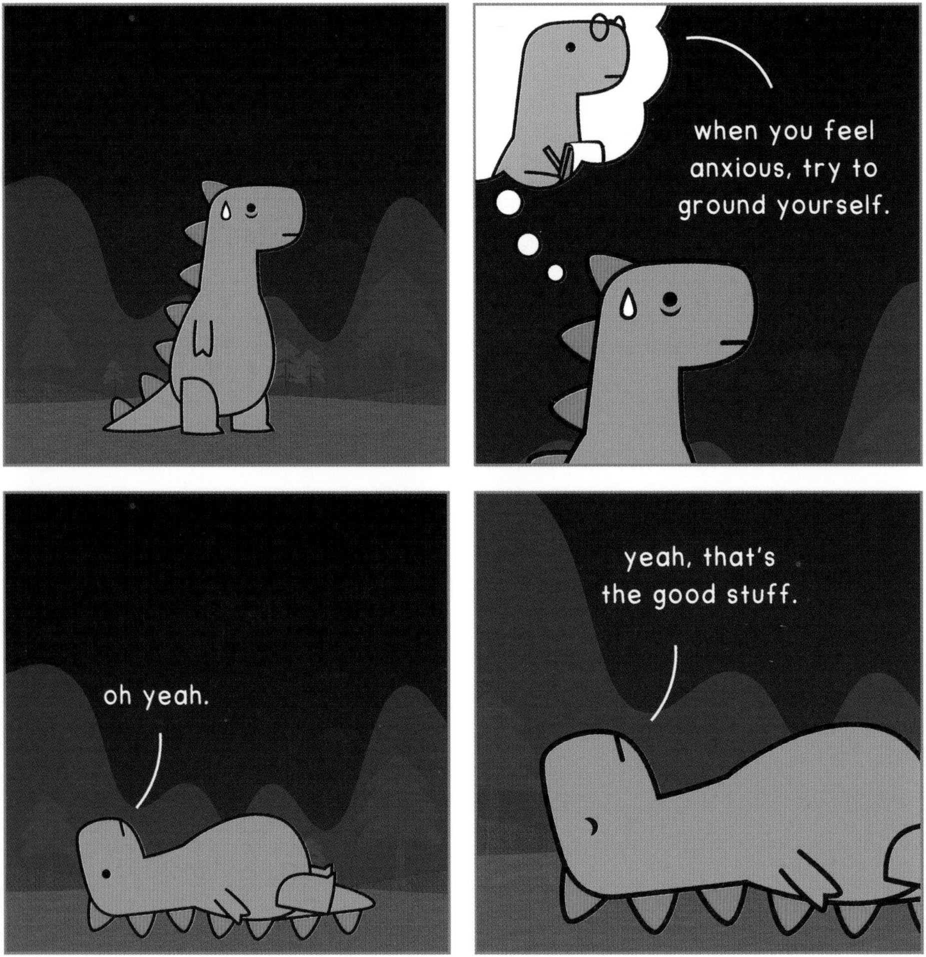
when you feel anxious, try to ground yourself.
oh yeah.
yeah, that's the good stuff.

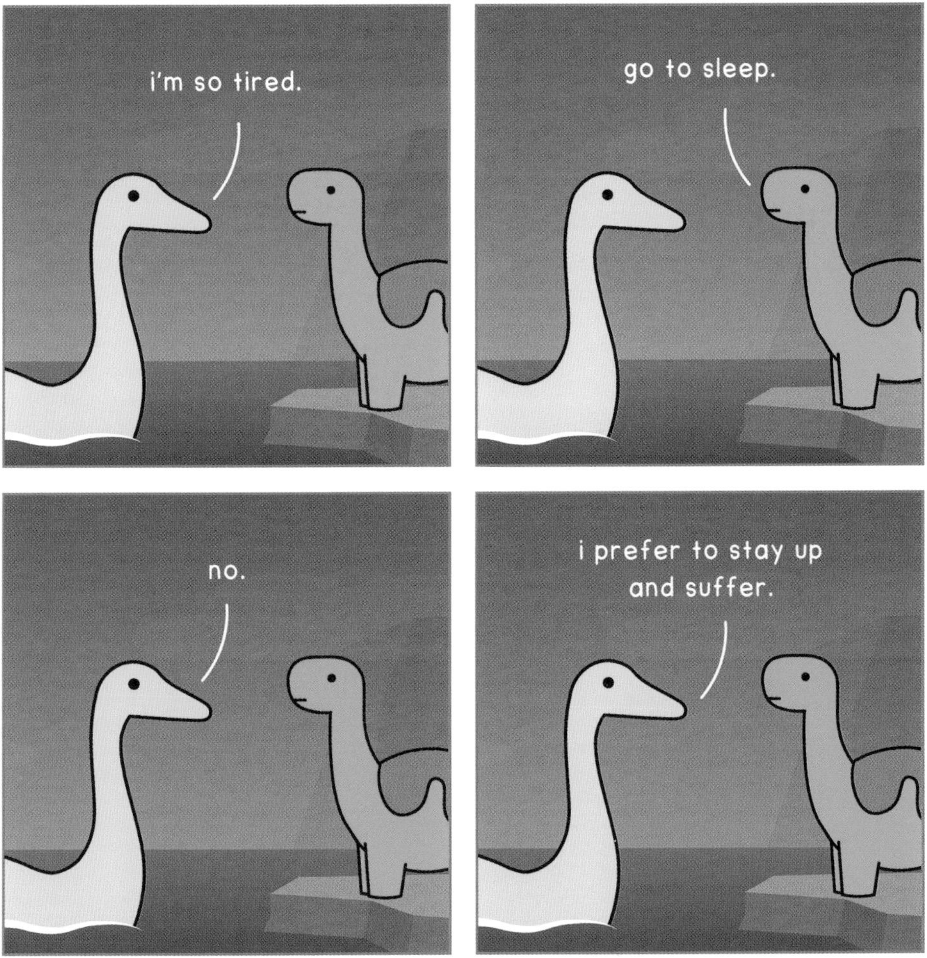
i'm so tired.
go to sleep.
no.
i prefer to stay up and suffer.

ethics

how should i live?

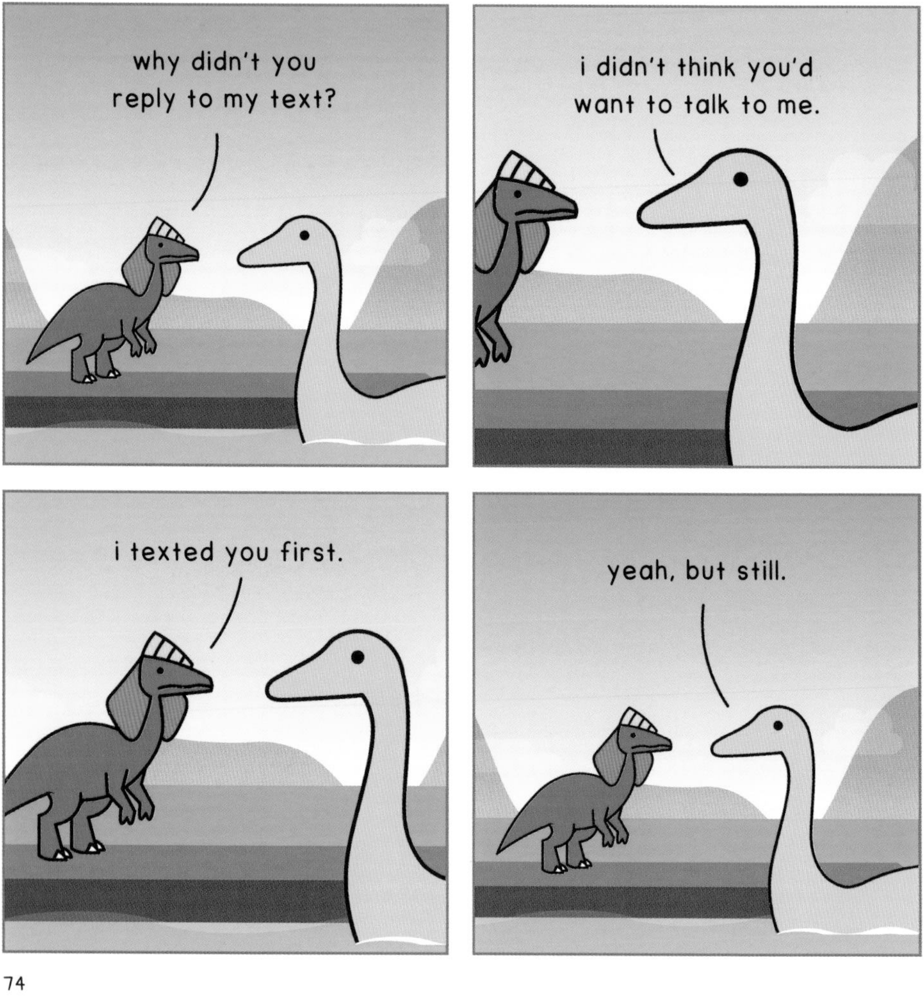
why didn't you reply to my text?
i didn't think you'd want to talk to me.
i texted you first.
yeah, but still.

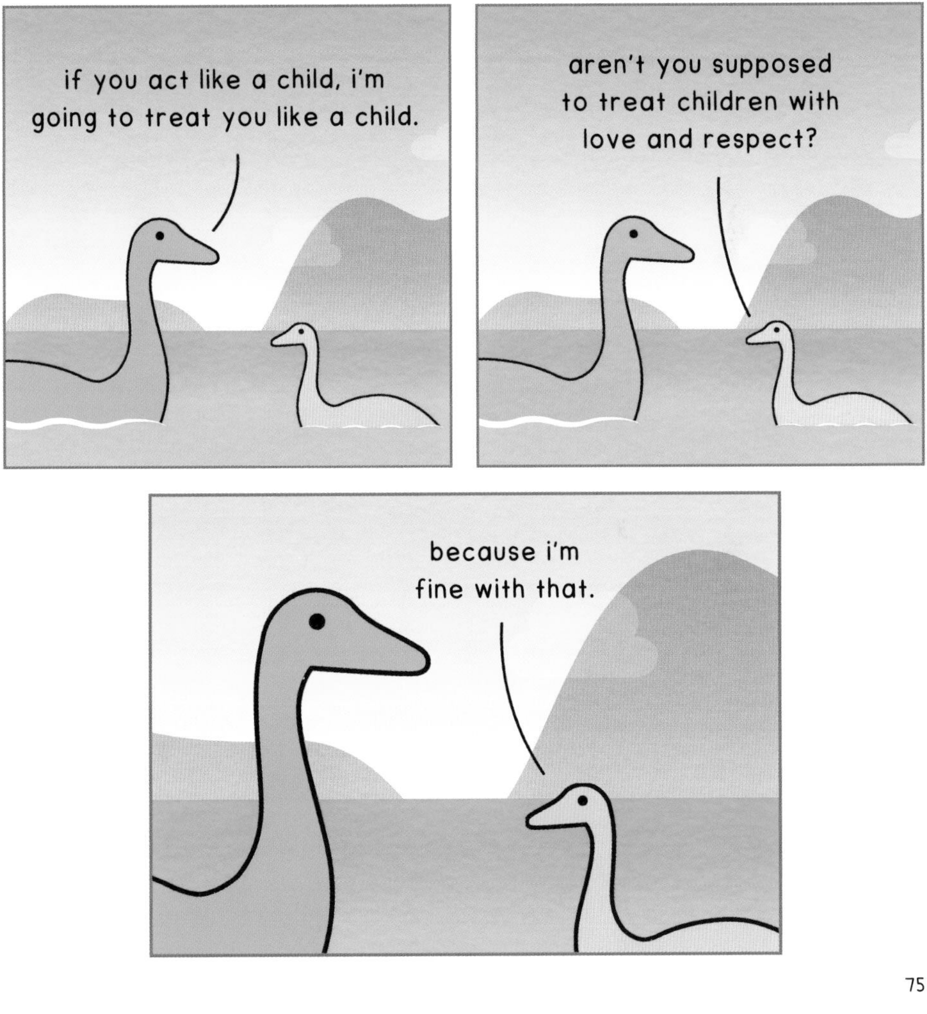
if you act like a child, i'm going to treat you like a child.
aren't you supposed to treat children with love and respect?
because i'm fine with that.

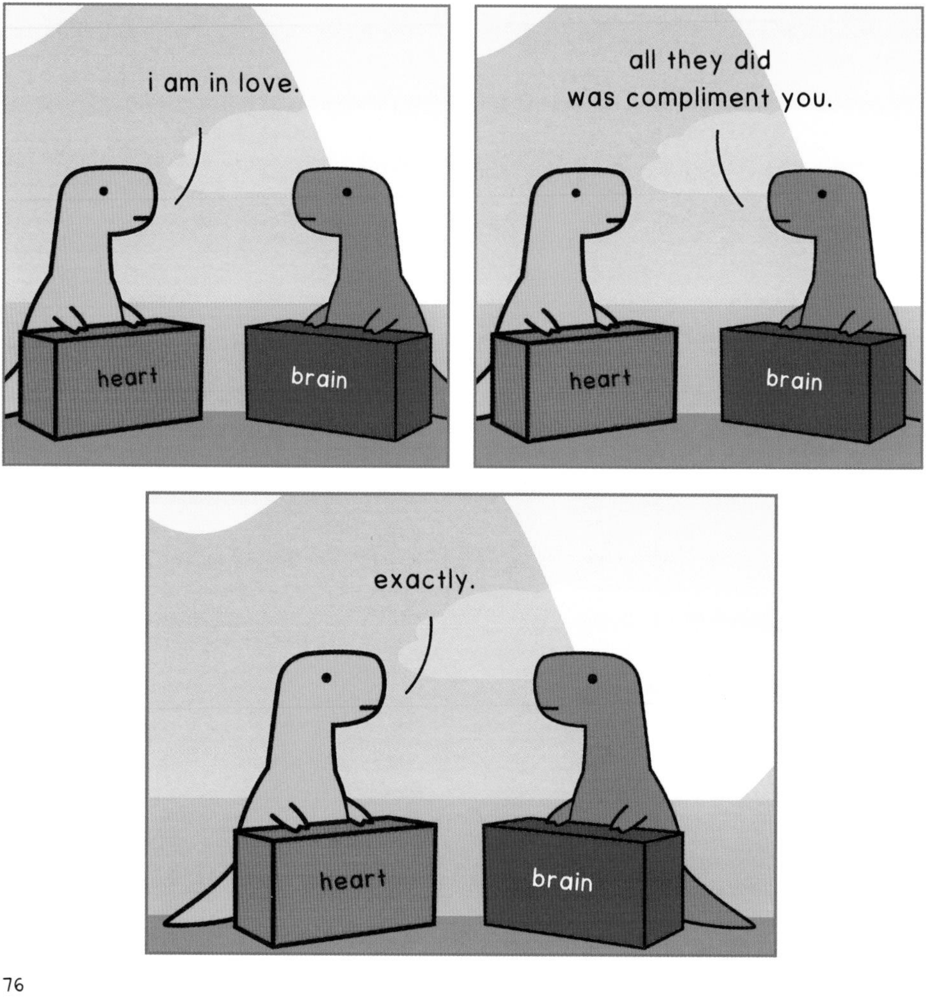
i am in love.
heart
brain
all they did
was compliment you.
heart
brain
exactly.
heart
brain

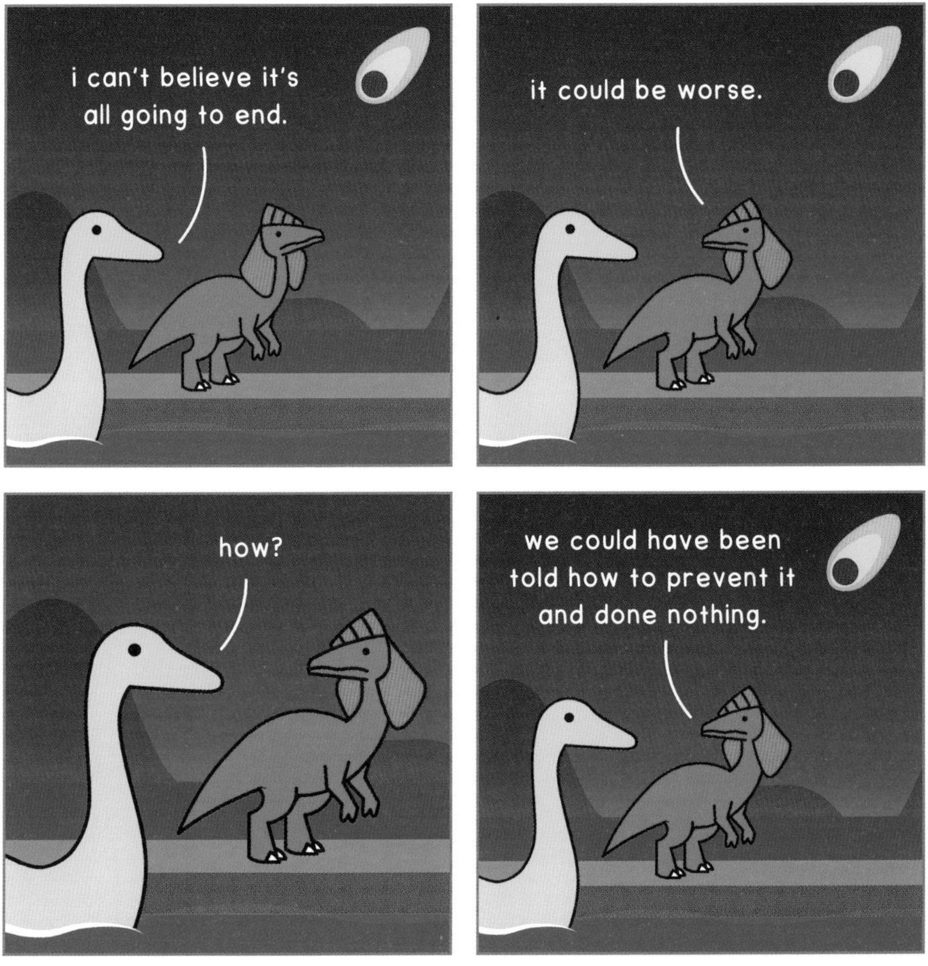

i can't believe it's all going to end.
it could be worse.
how?
we could have been told how to prevent it and done nothing.

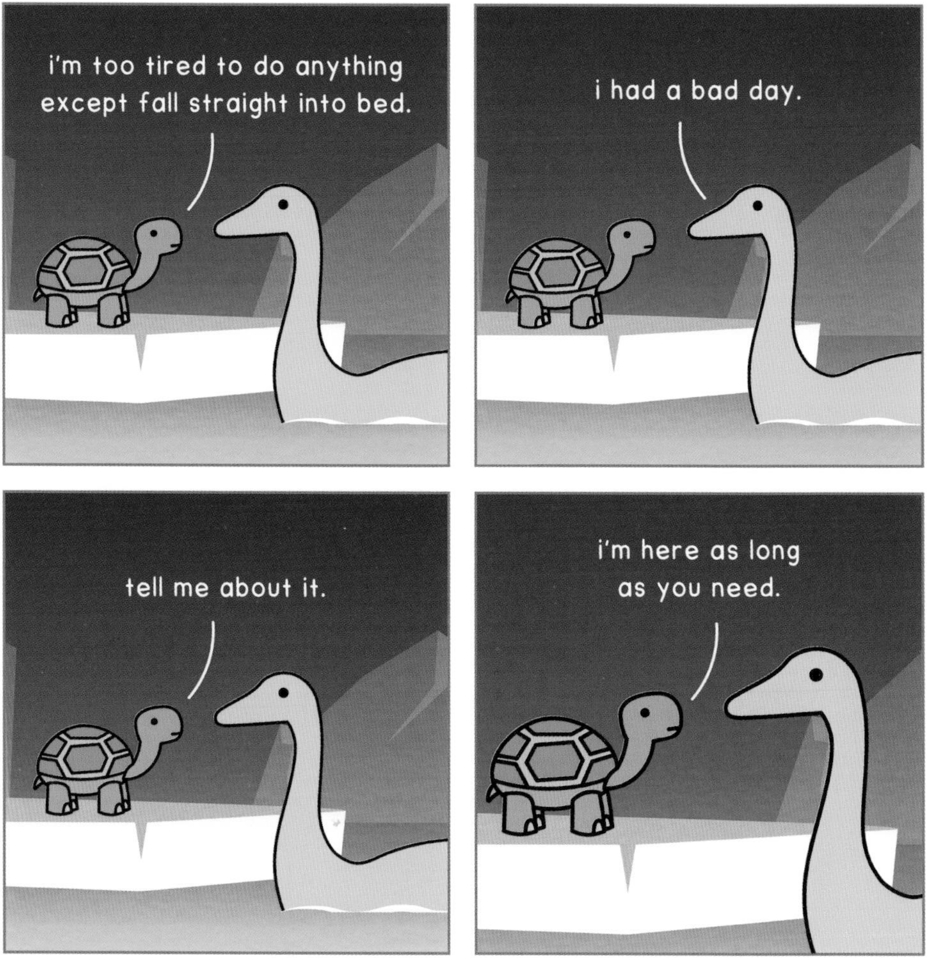
i'm too tired to do anything except fall straight into bed.
i had a bad day.
tell me about it.
i'm here as long as you need.

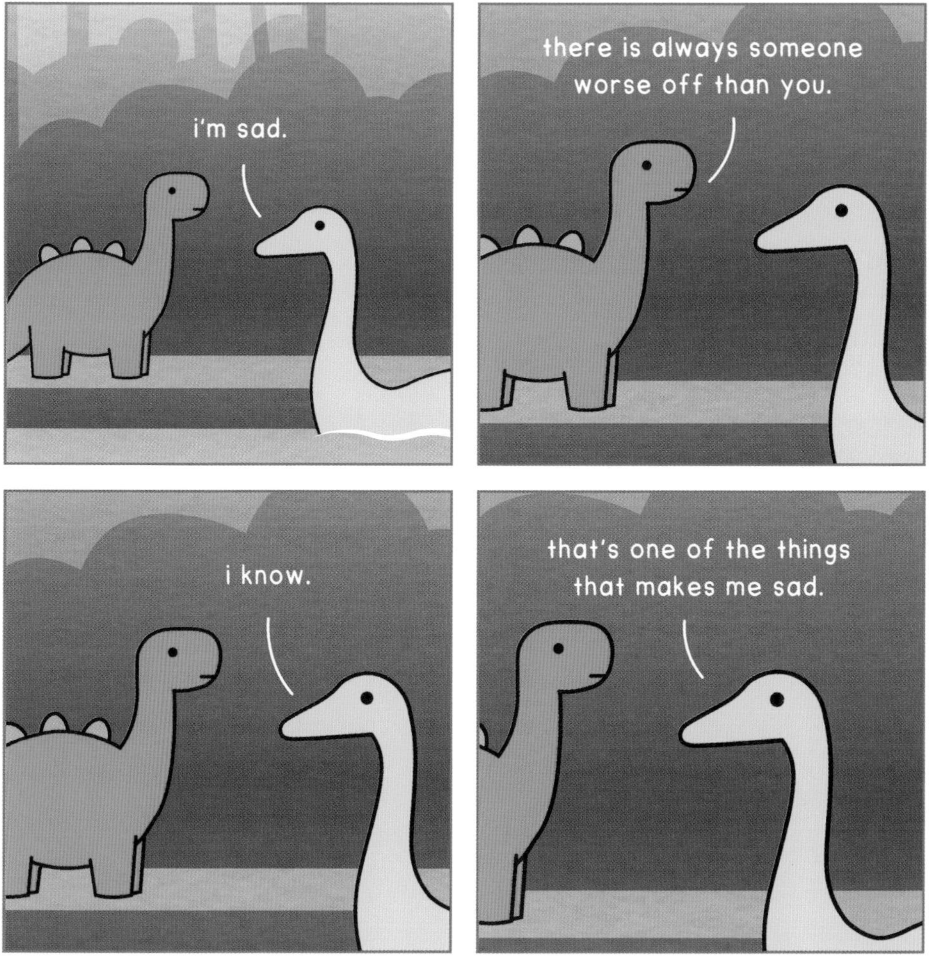
i'm sad.
there is always someone worse off than you.
i know.
that's one of the things that makes me sad.

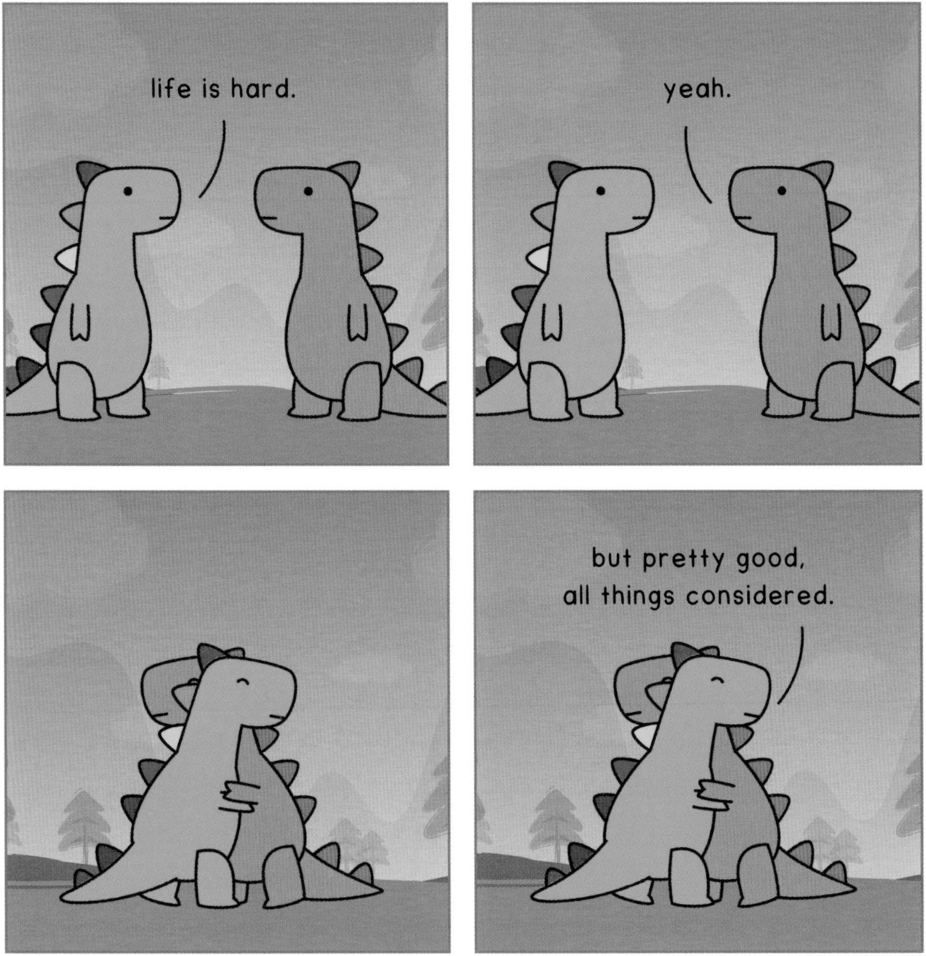
life is hard.
yeah.
but pretty good,
all things considered.

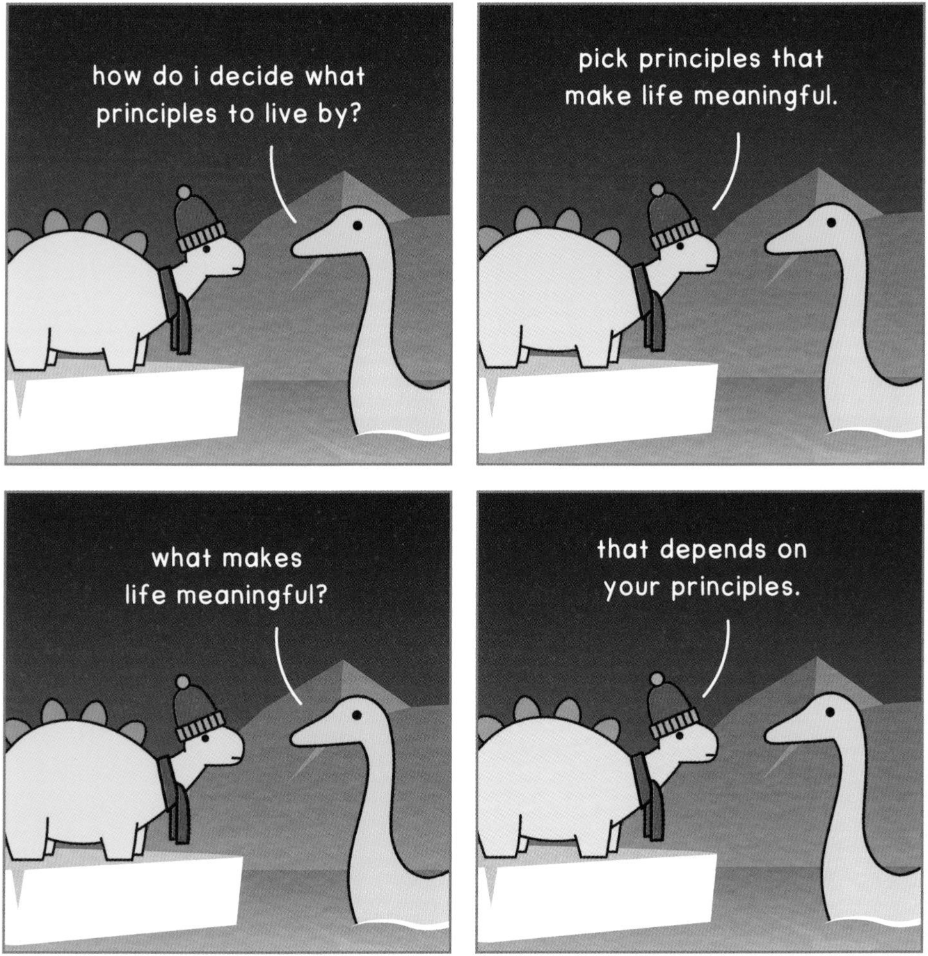
how do i decide what principles to live by?
pick principles that make life meaningful.
what makes life meaningful?
that depends on your principles.

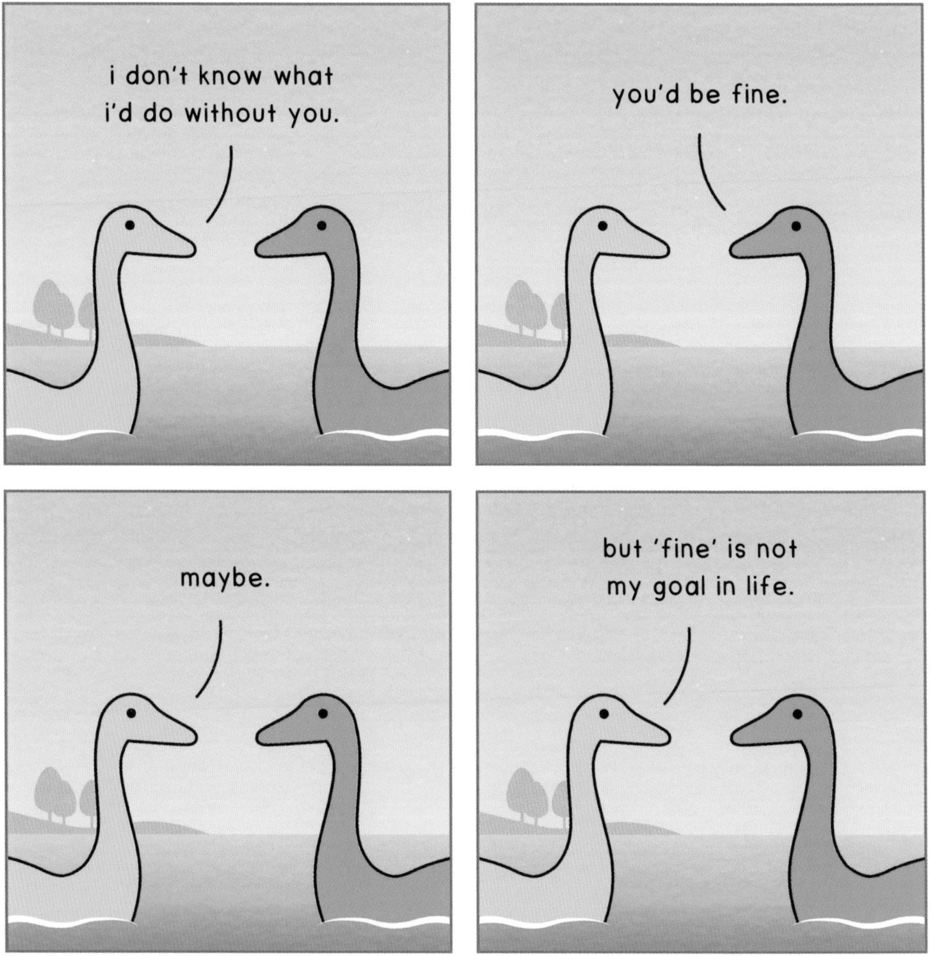
i don't know what i'd do without you.
you'd be fine.
maybe.
but 'fine' is not my goal in life.

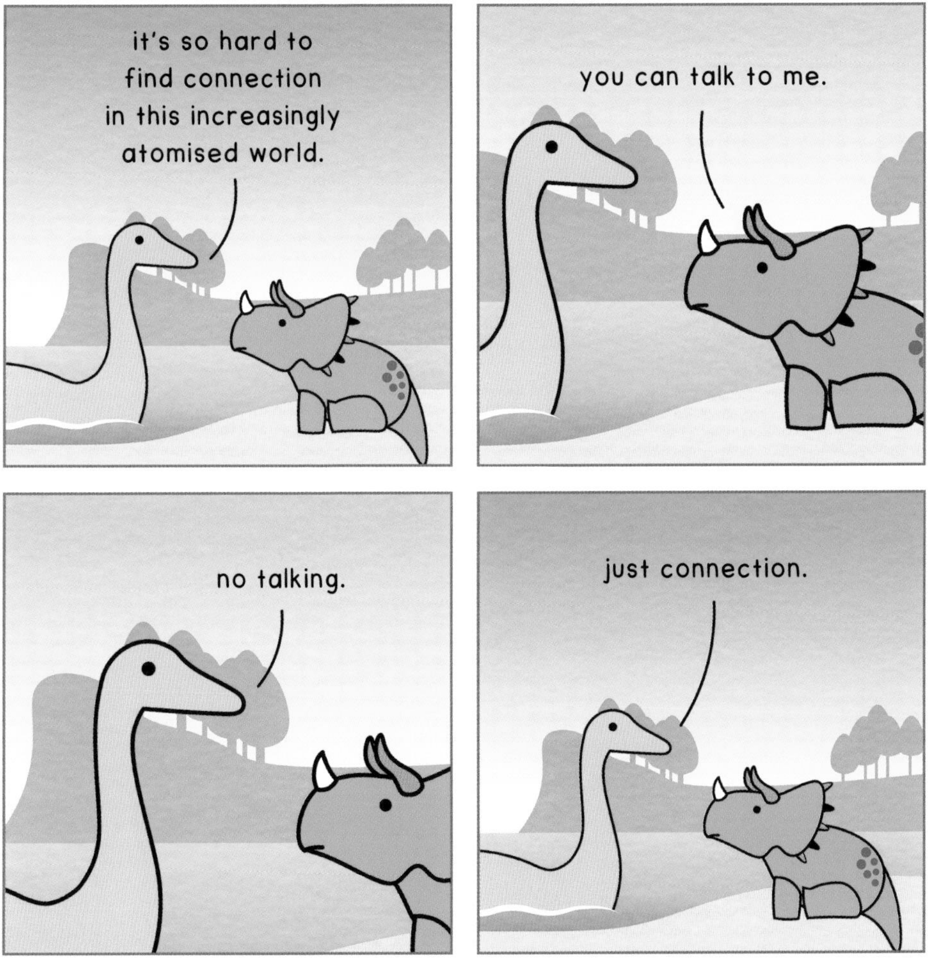
it's so hard to find connection in this increasingly atomised world.
you can talk to me.
no talking.
just connection.

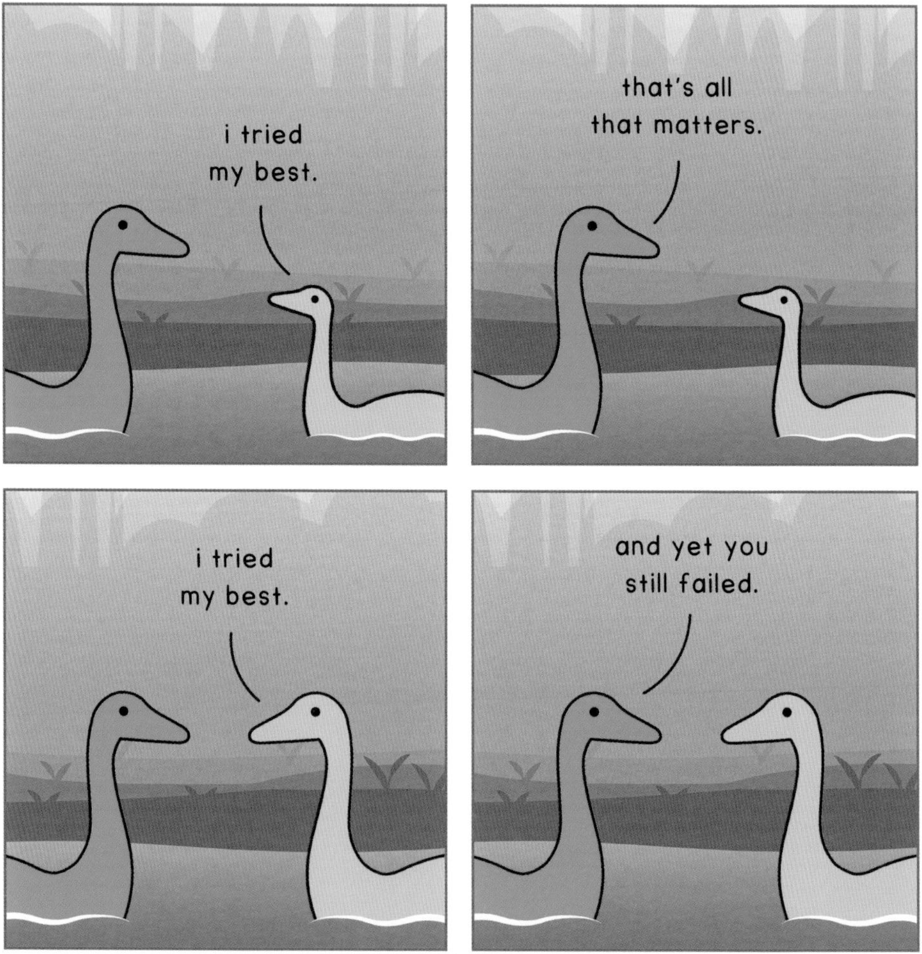
i tried my best.
that's all that matters.
i tried my best.
and yet you still failed.

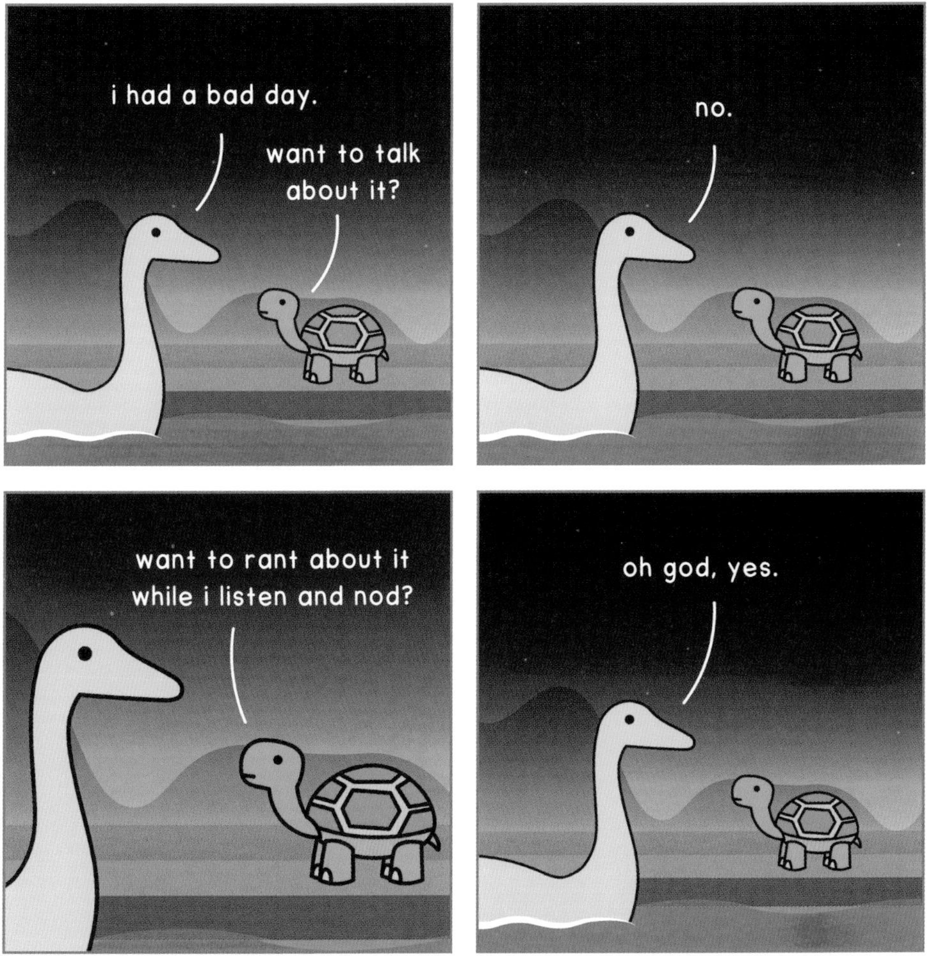
i had a bad day.
want to talk about it?
no.
want to rant about it while i listen and nod?
oh god, yes.

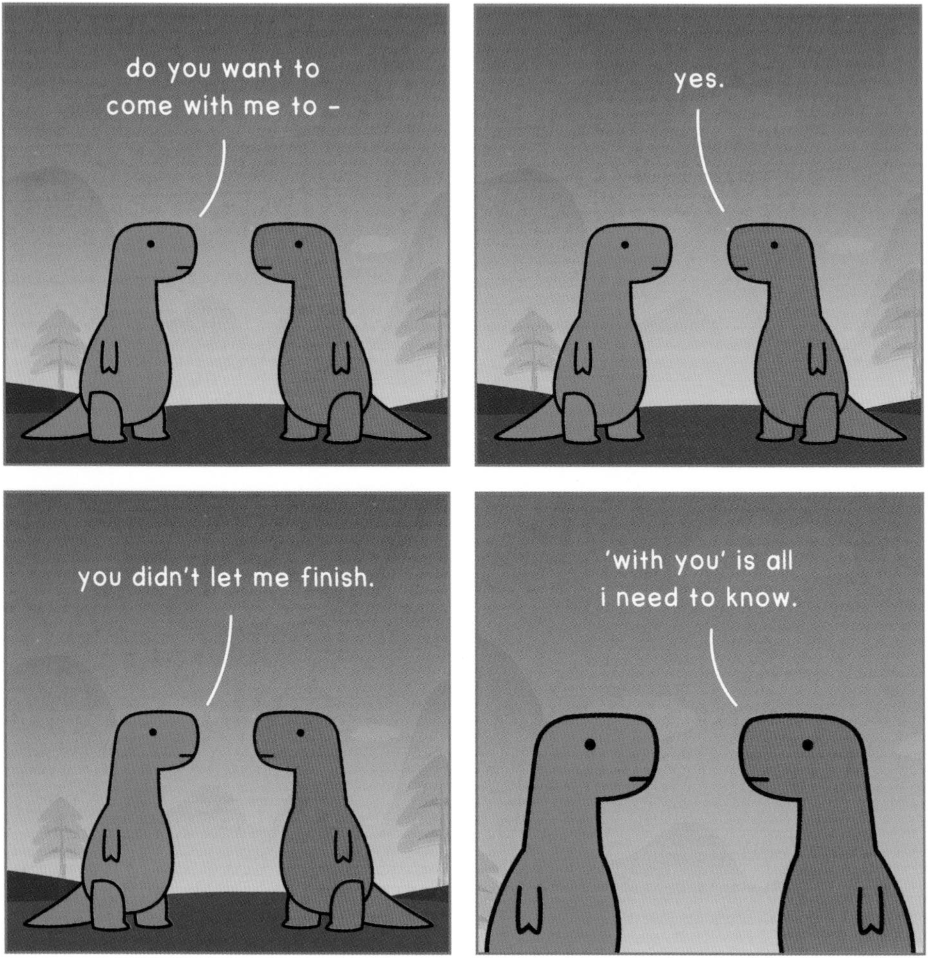
do you want to
come with me to -
yes.
you didn't let me finish.
'with you' is all
i need to know.

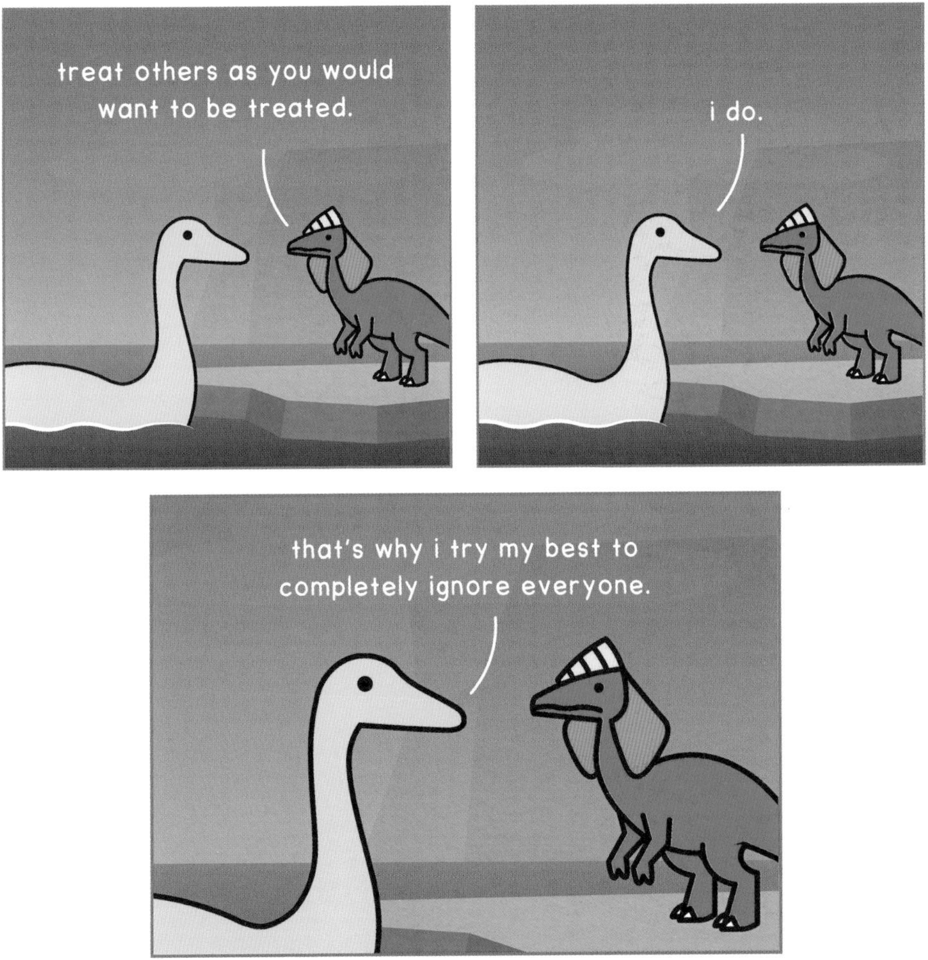
treat others as you would want to be treated.
i do.
that's why i try my best to completely ignore everyone.

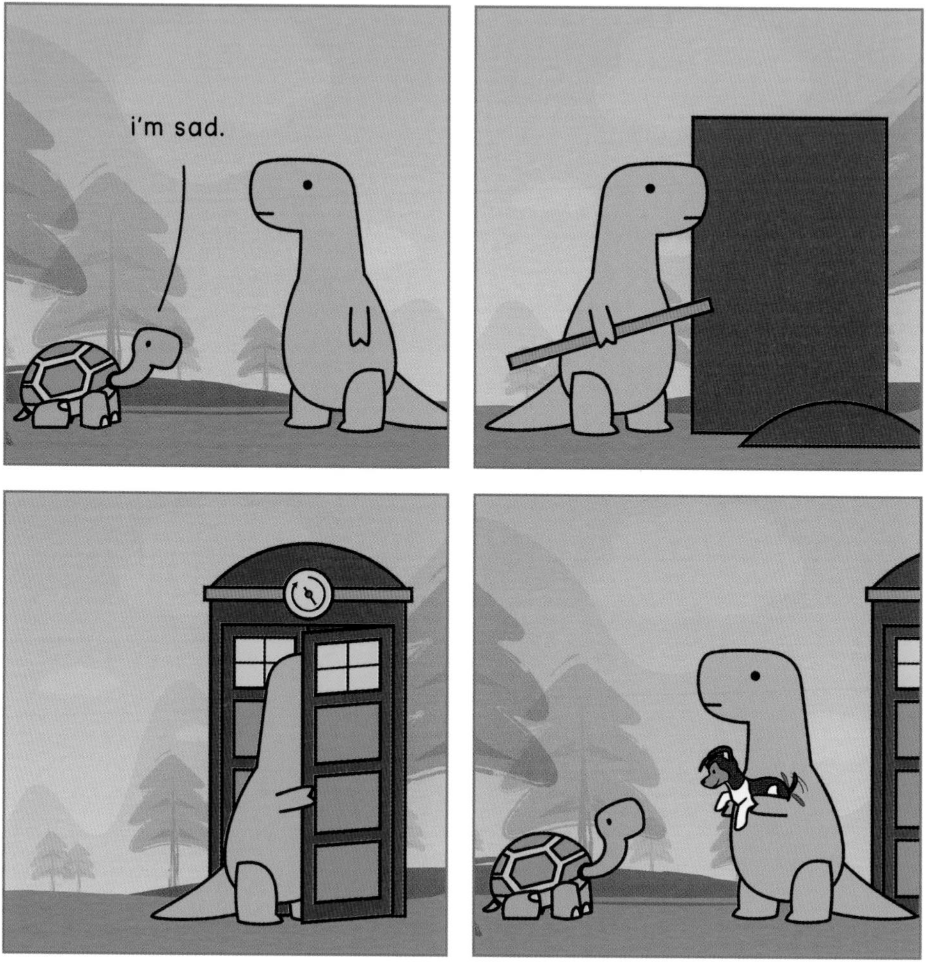
i'm sad.

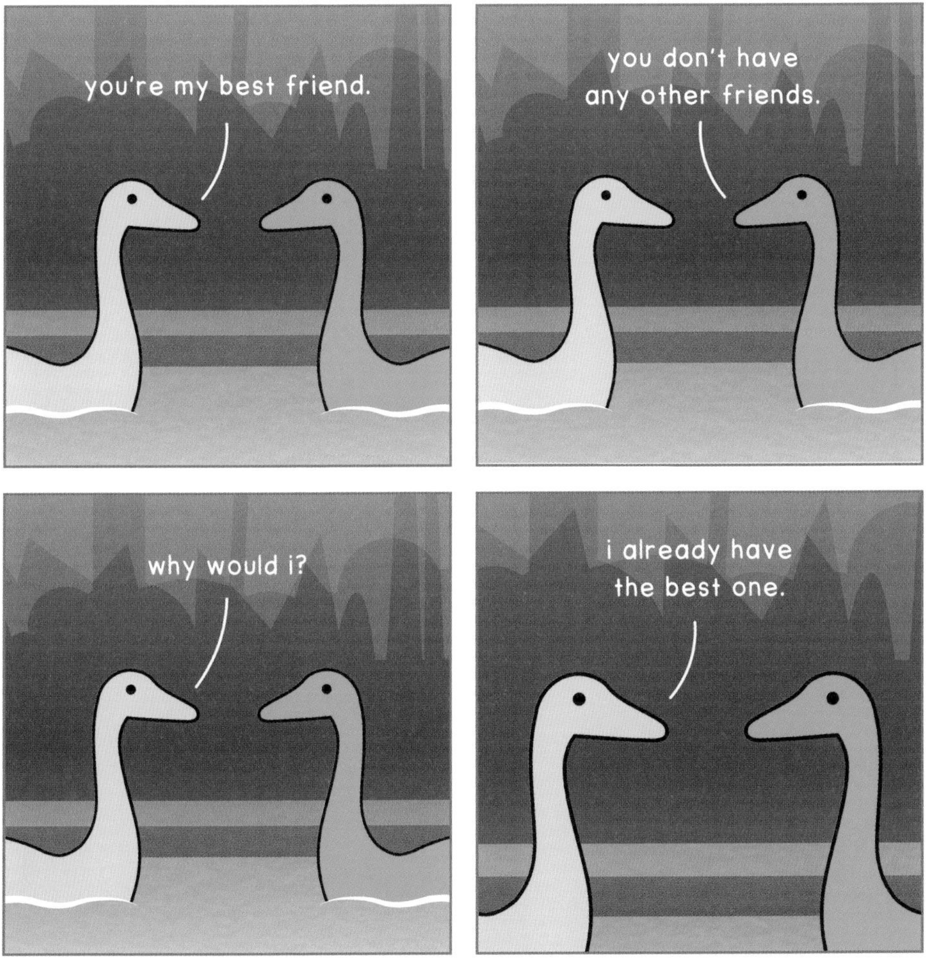
you're my best friend.
you don't have any other friends.
why would i?
i already have the best one.

i don't know what i'd do if i lost you.
really?
i know exactly what i'd do.
what?
find you.

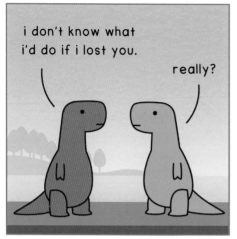

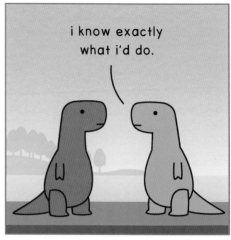

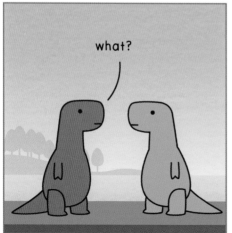

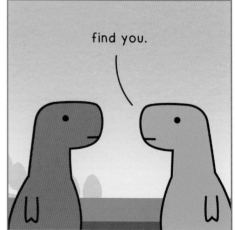

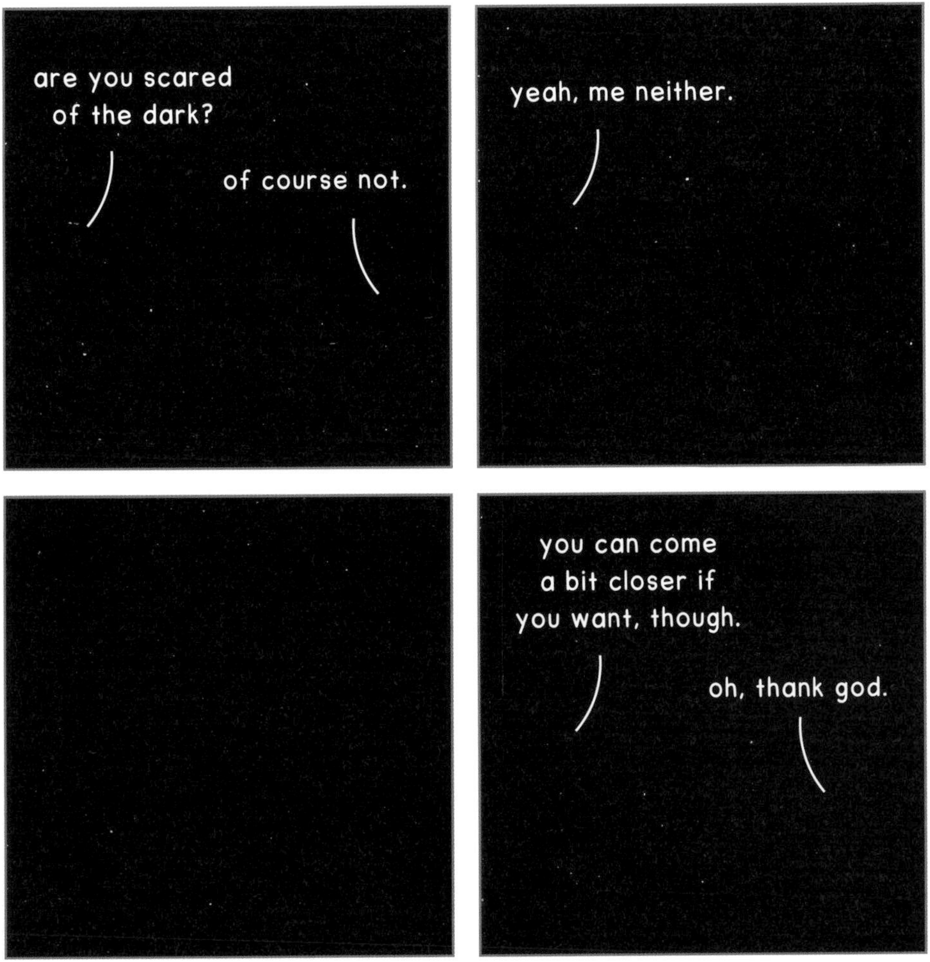
are you scared of the dark?
of course not.
yeah, me neither.
you can come a bit closer if you want, though.
oh, thank god.

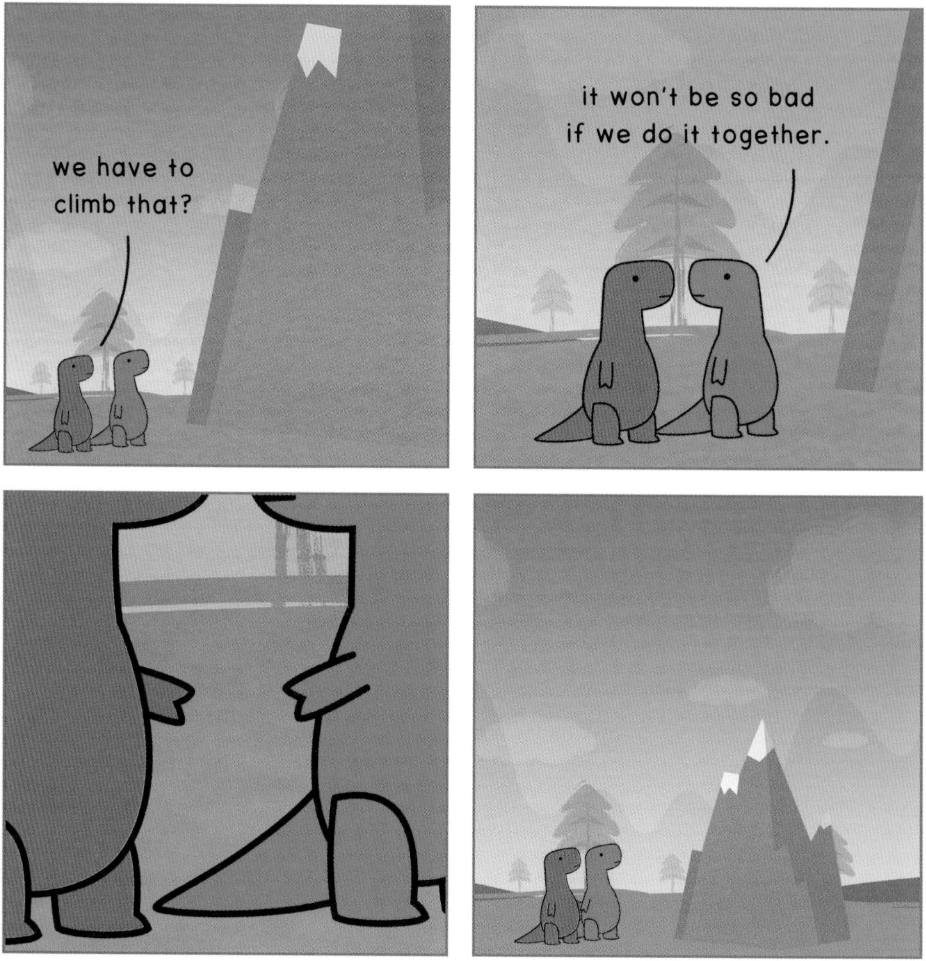
we have to climb that?
it won't be so bad if we do it together.

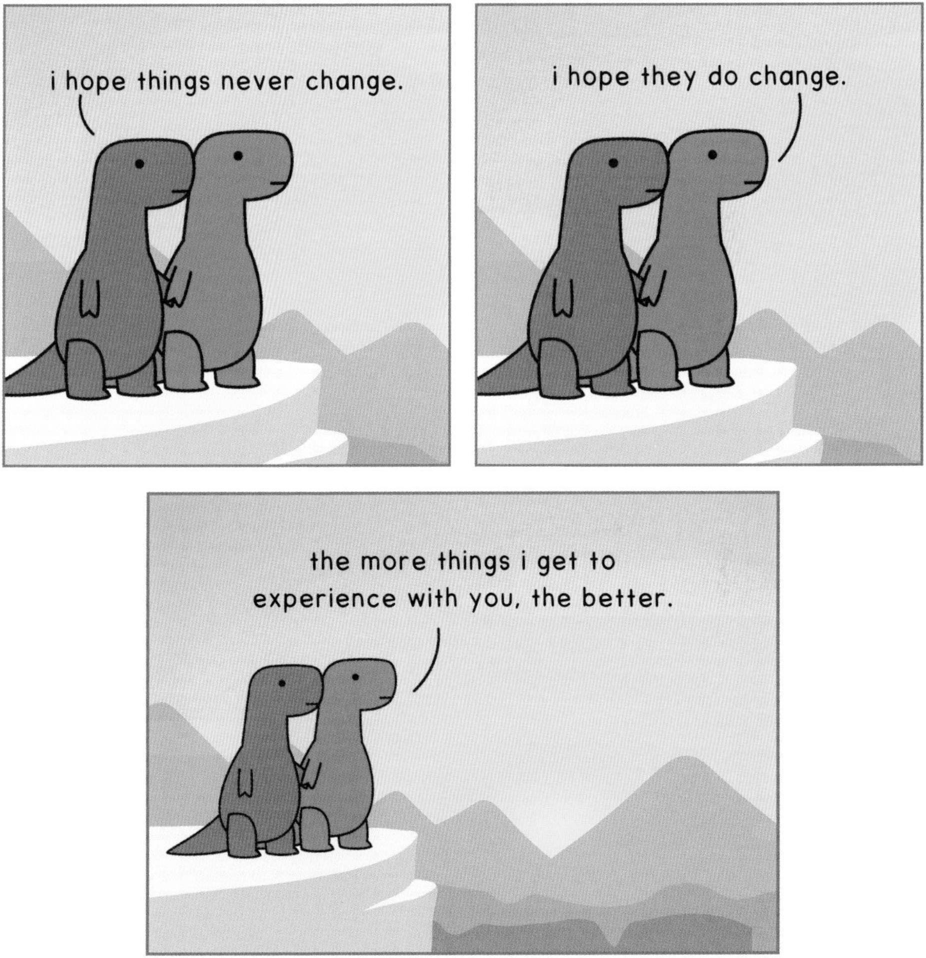
i hope things never change.
i hope they do change.
the more things i get to experience with you, the better.

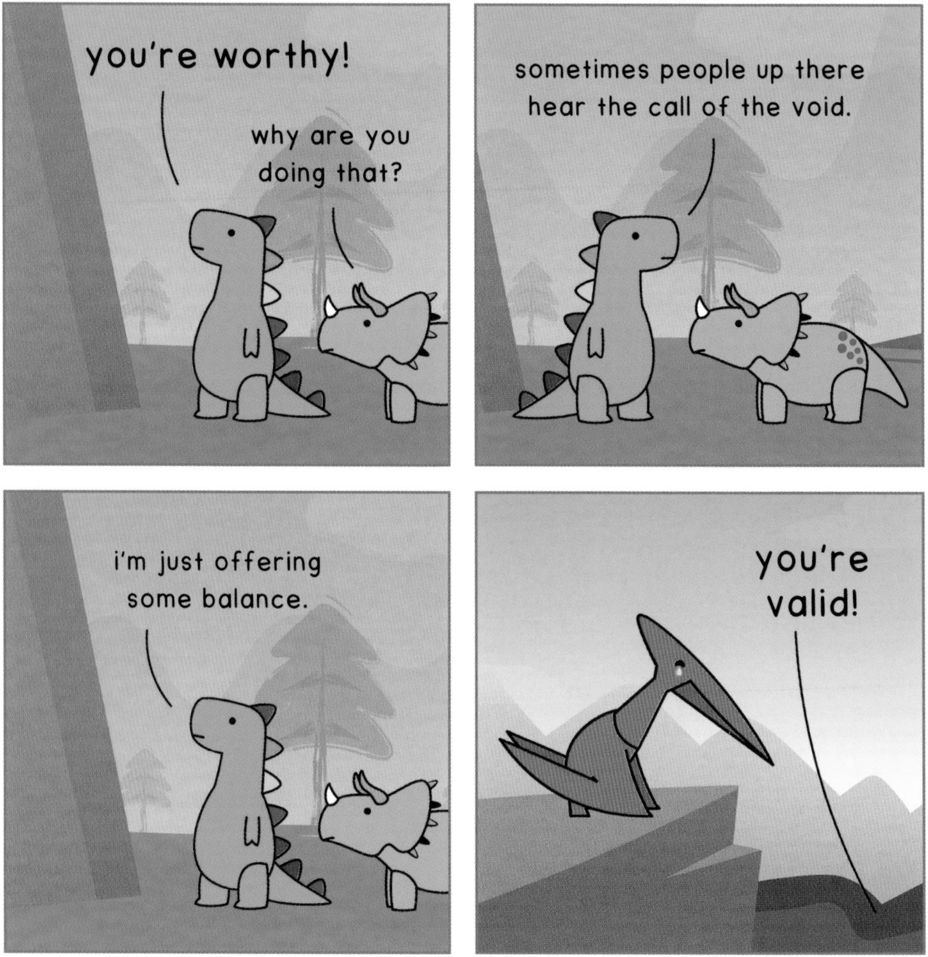
you're worthy!
why are you doing that?
sometimes people up there hear the call of the void.
i'm just offering some balance.
you're valid!

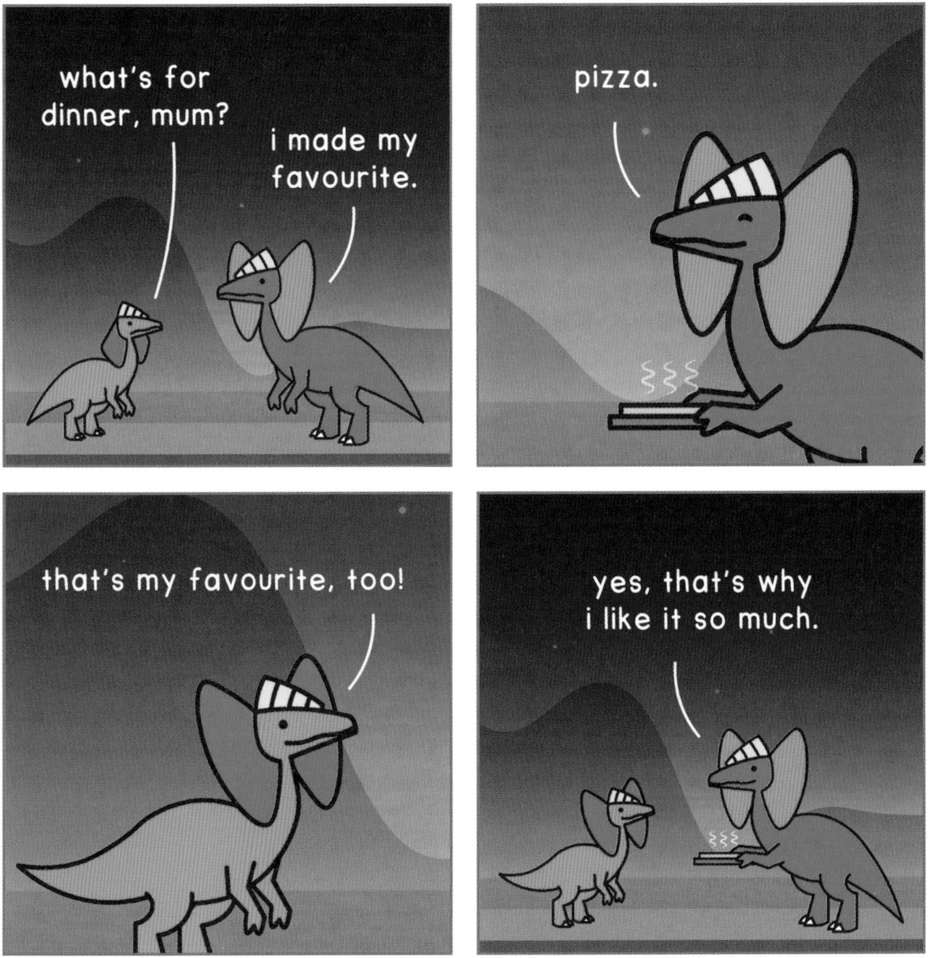
what's for dinner, mum?
i made my favourite.
pizza.
that's my favourite, too!
yes, that's why i like it so much.

political philosophy

how should
we live?

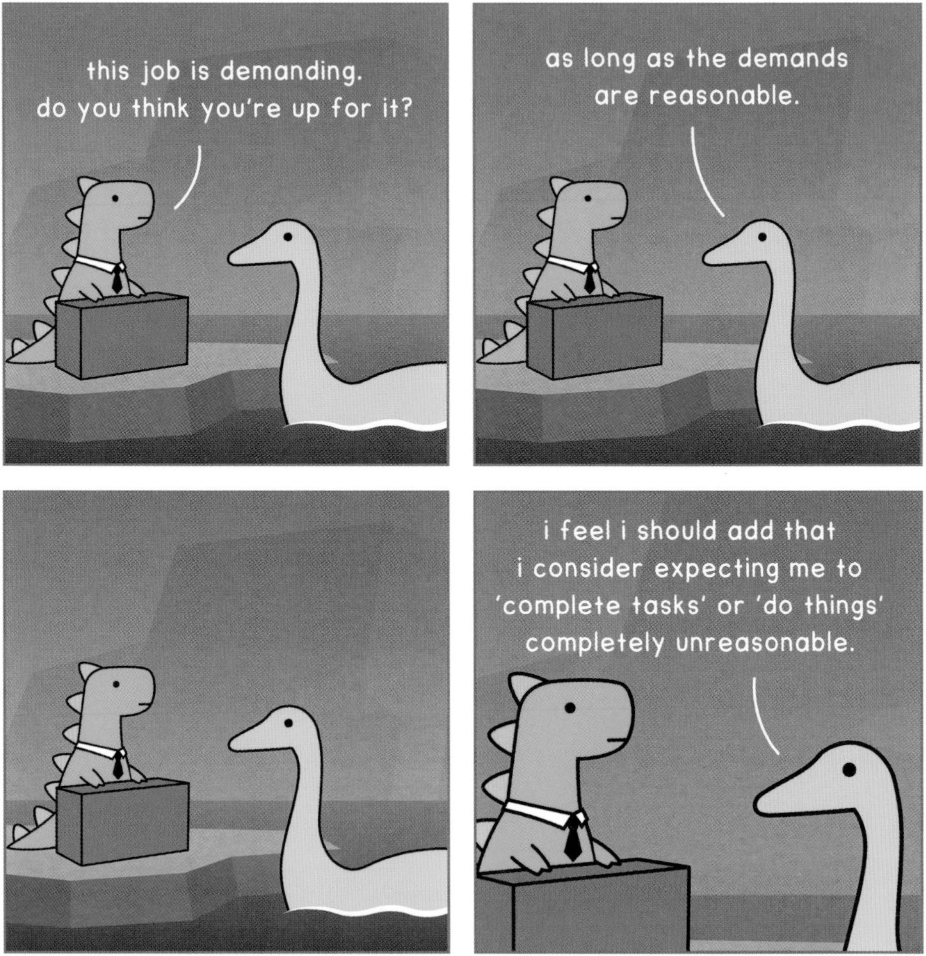
this job is demanding.
do you think you're up for it?
as long as the demands
are reasonable.
i feel i should add that
i consider expecting me to
'complete tasks' or 'do things'
completely unreasonable.

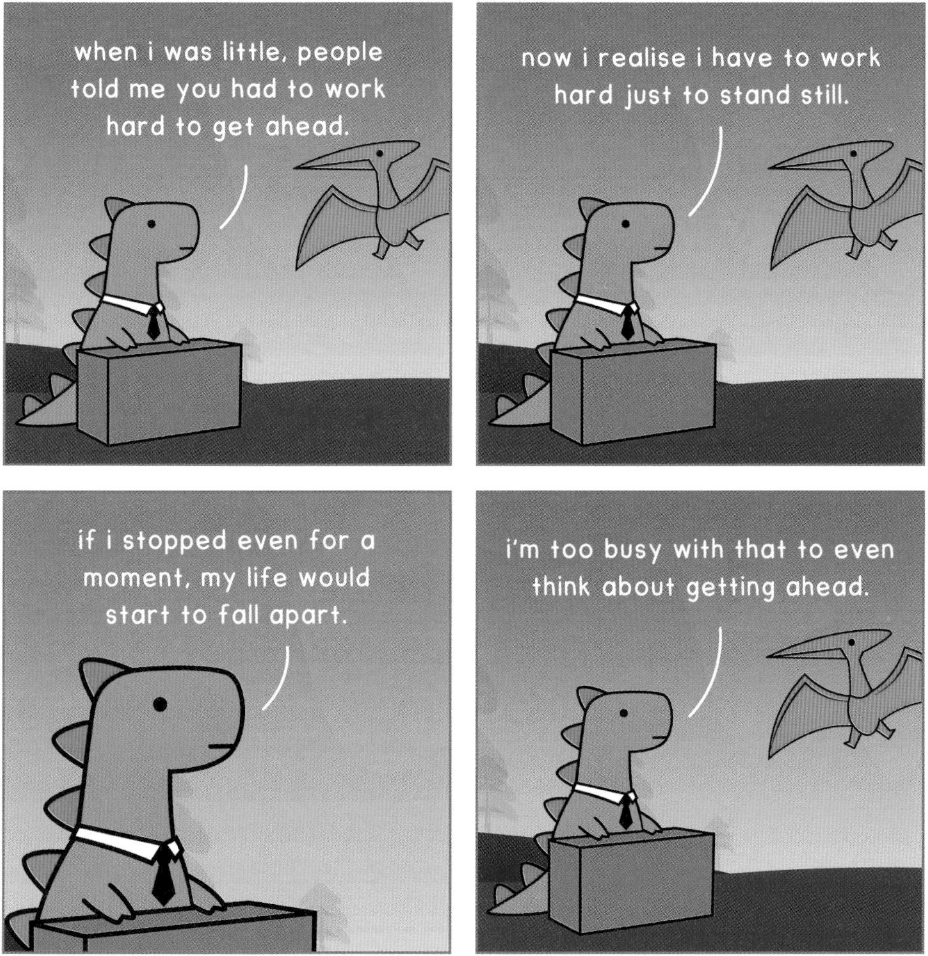
when i was little, people told me you had to work hard to get ahead.
now i realise i have to work hard just to stand still.
if i stopped even for a moment, my life would start to fall apart.
i'm too busy with that to even think about getting ahead.

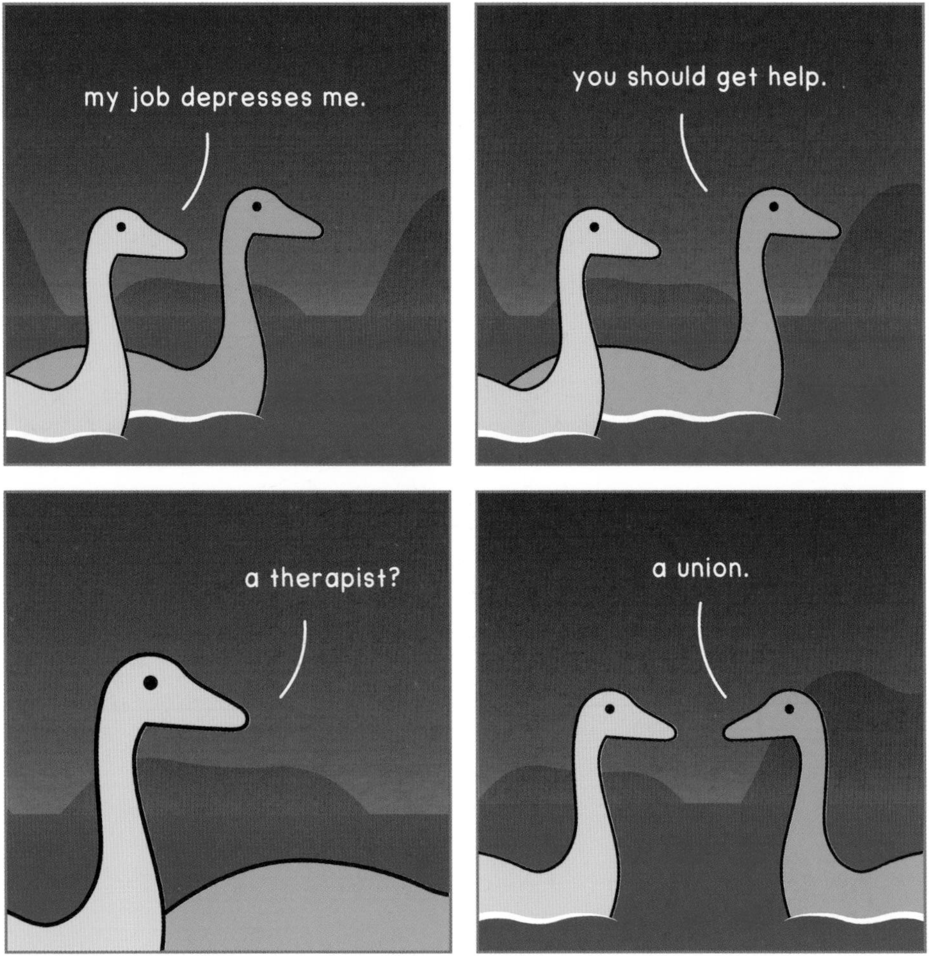
my job depresses me.
you should get help.
a therapist?
a union.

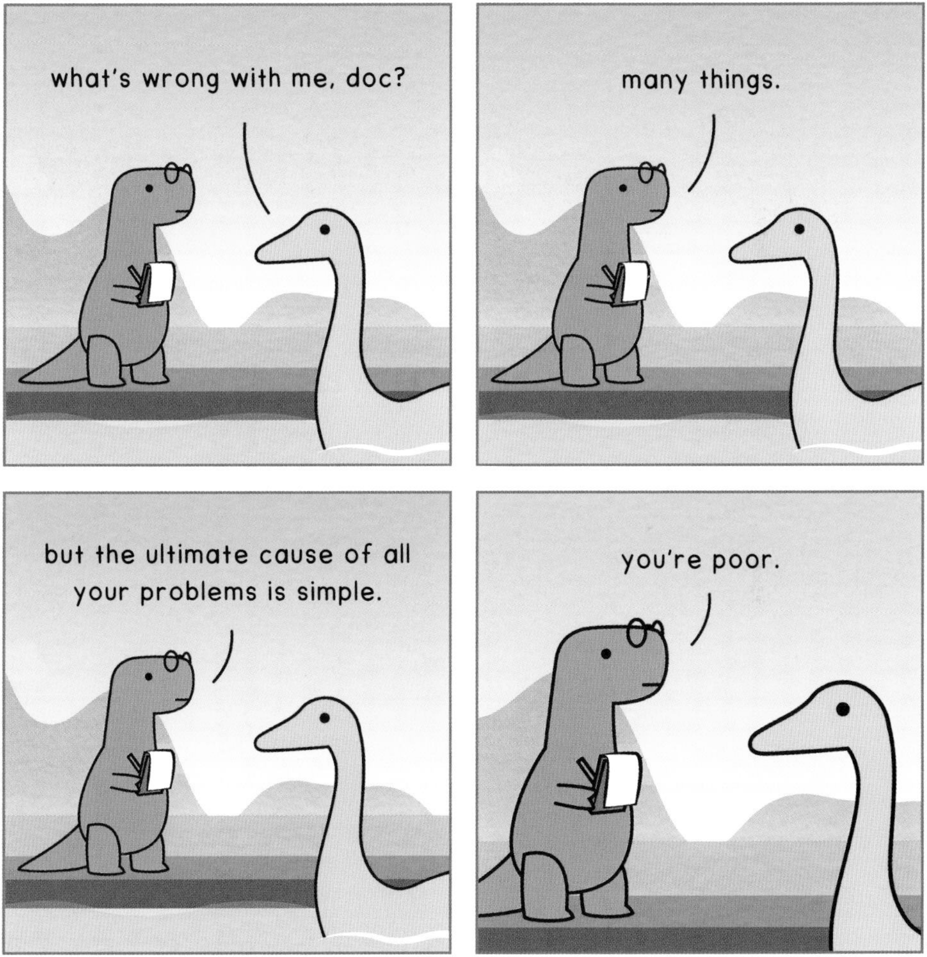
what's wrong with me, doc?
many things.
but the ultimate cause of all your problems is simple.
you're poor.

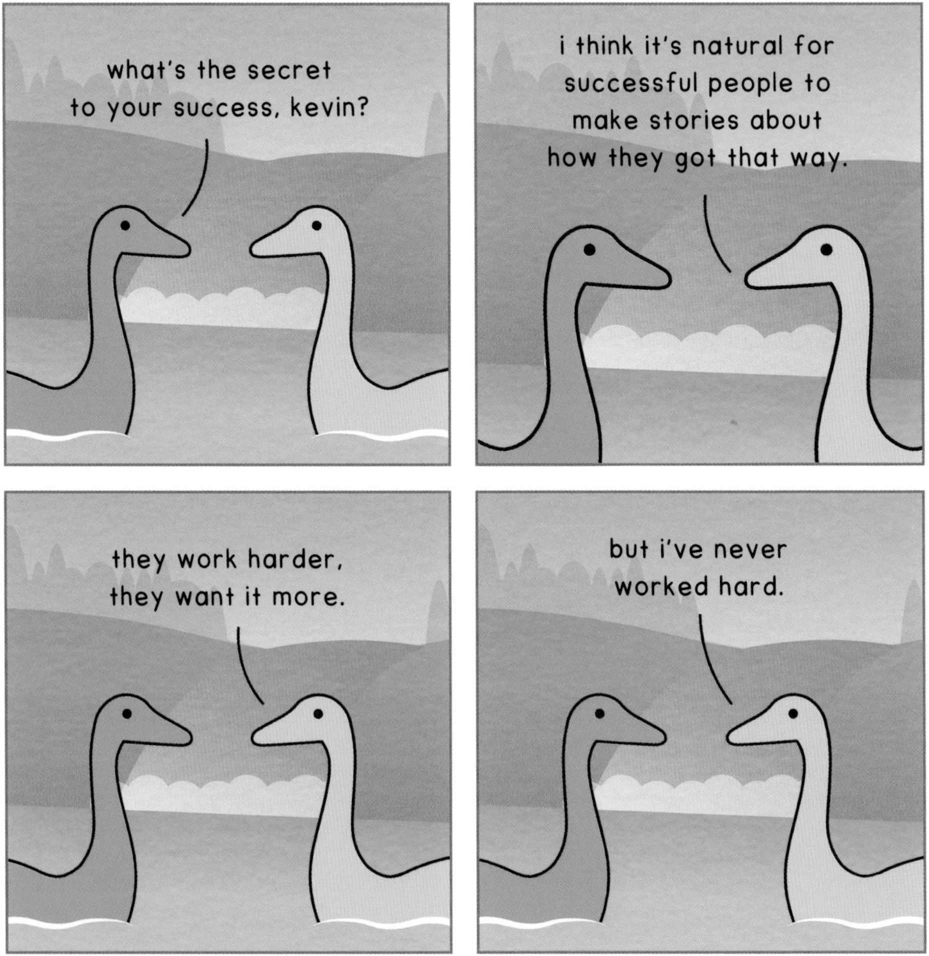
what's the secret to your success, kevin?
i think it's natural for successful people to make stories about how they got that way.
they work harder, they want it more.
but i've never worked hard.

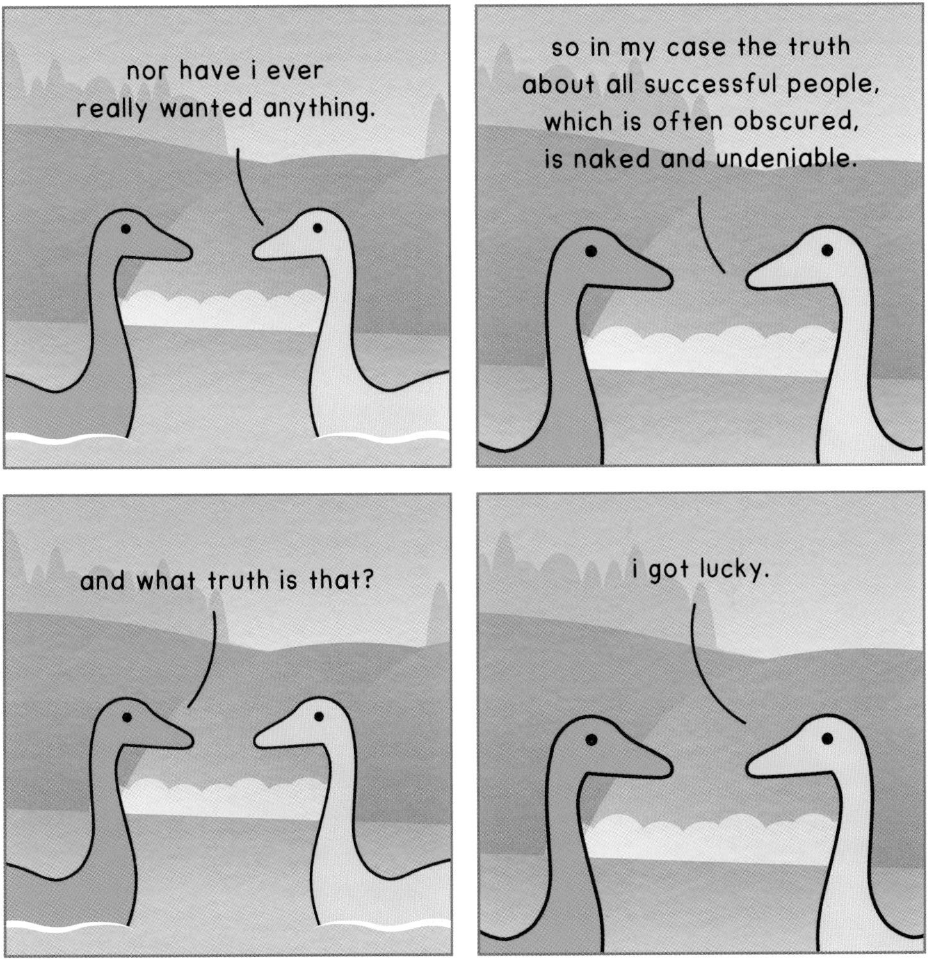
nor have i ever really wanted anything.
so in my case the truth about all successful people, which is often obscured, is naked and undeniable.
and what truth is that?
i got lucky.

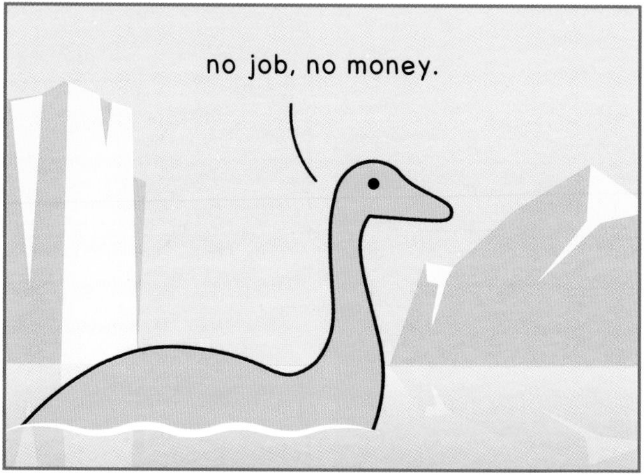
no job, no money.

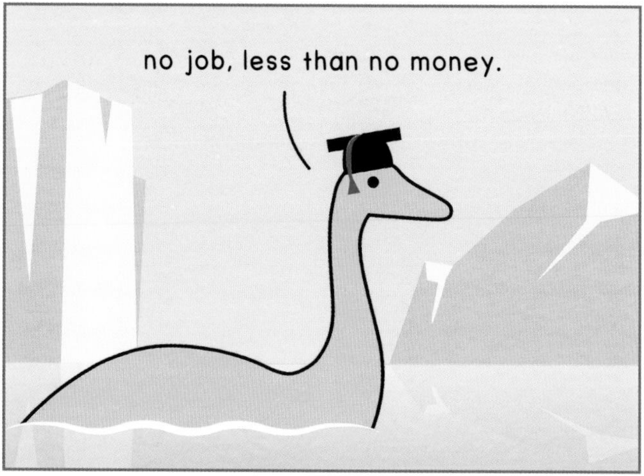
no job, less than no money.

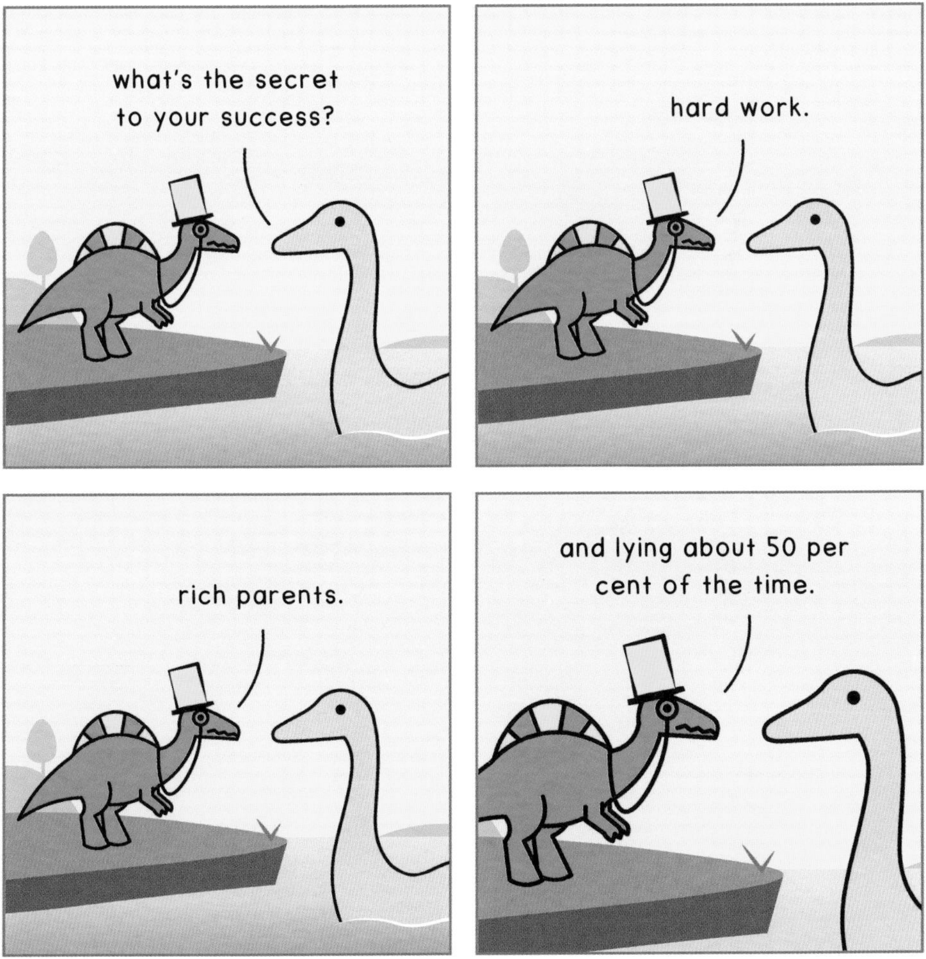
what's the secret to your success?
hard work.
rich parents.
and lying about 50 per cent of the time.

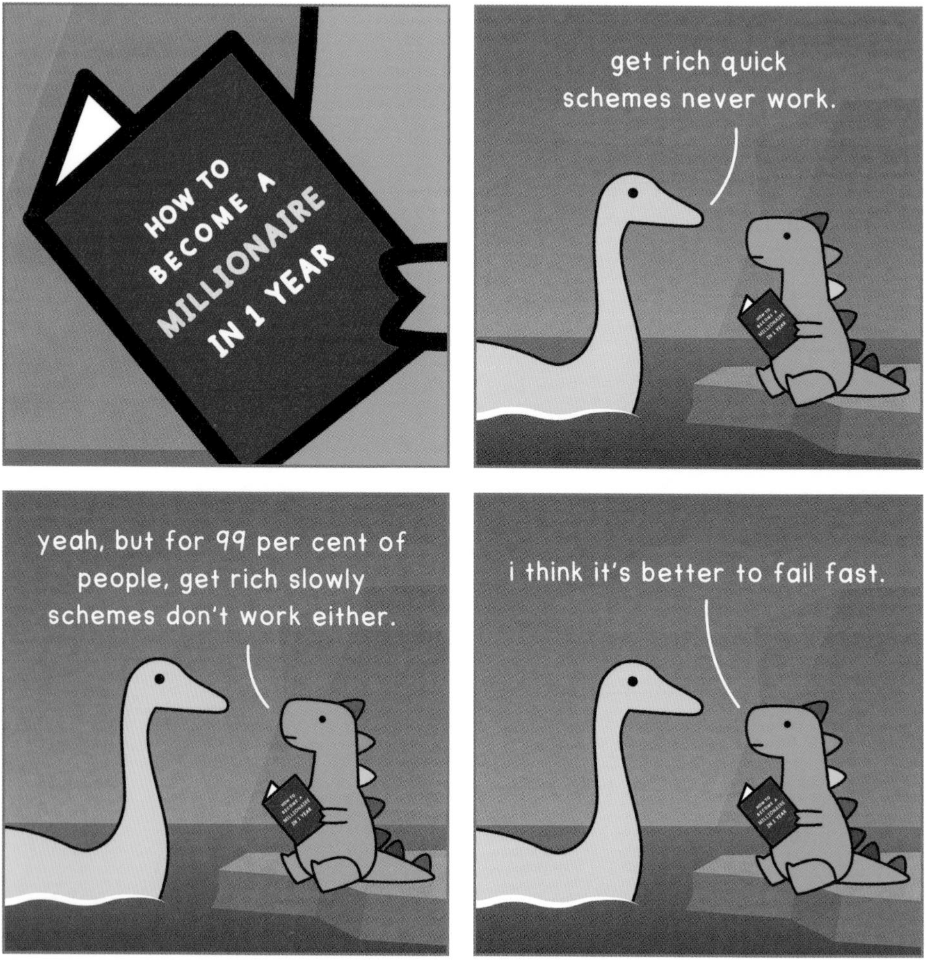
HOW TO BECOME A MILLIONAIRE IN 1 YEAR
get rich quick schemes never work.
yeah, but for 99 per cent of people, get rich slowly schemes don't work either.
i think it's better to fail fast.

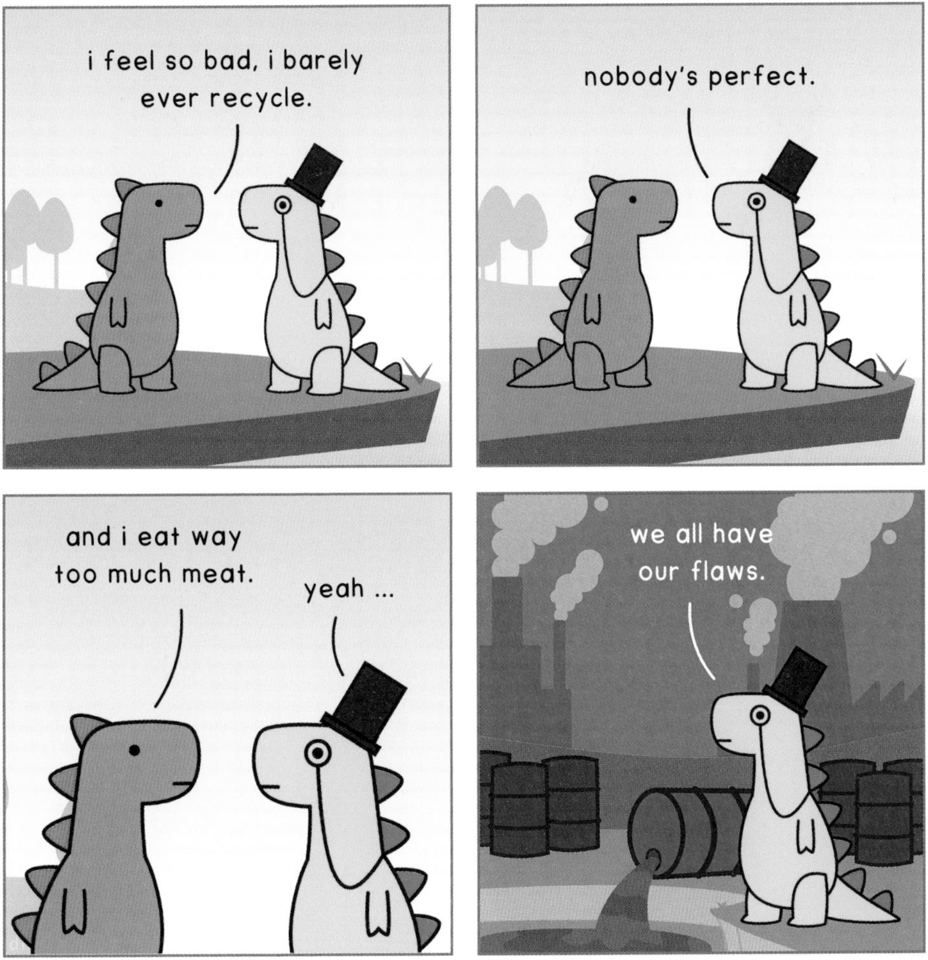
i feel so bad, i barely ever recycle.
nobody's perfect.
and i eat way too much meat.
yeah ...
we all have our flaws.

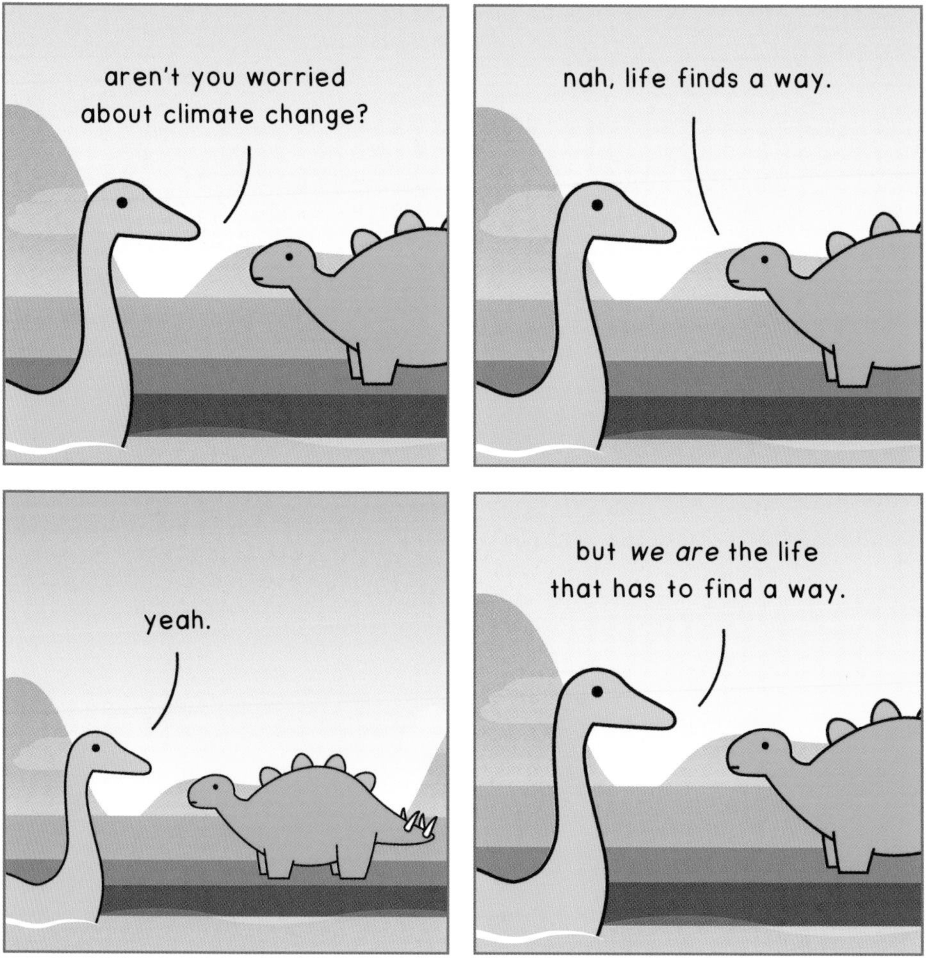
aren't you worried
about climate change?
nah, life finds a way.
yeah.
but *we are* the life
that has to find a way.

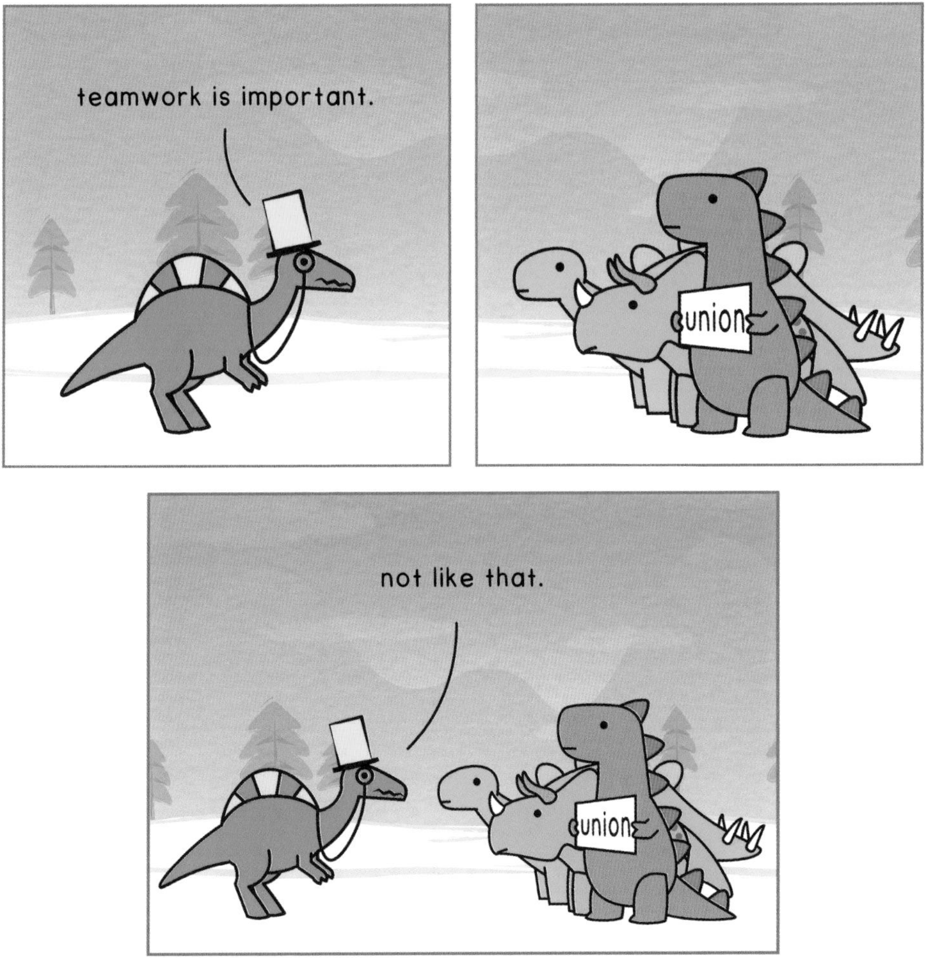
teamwork is important.
union
not like that.
union

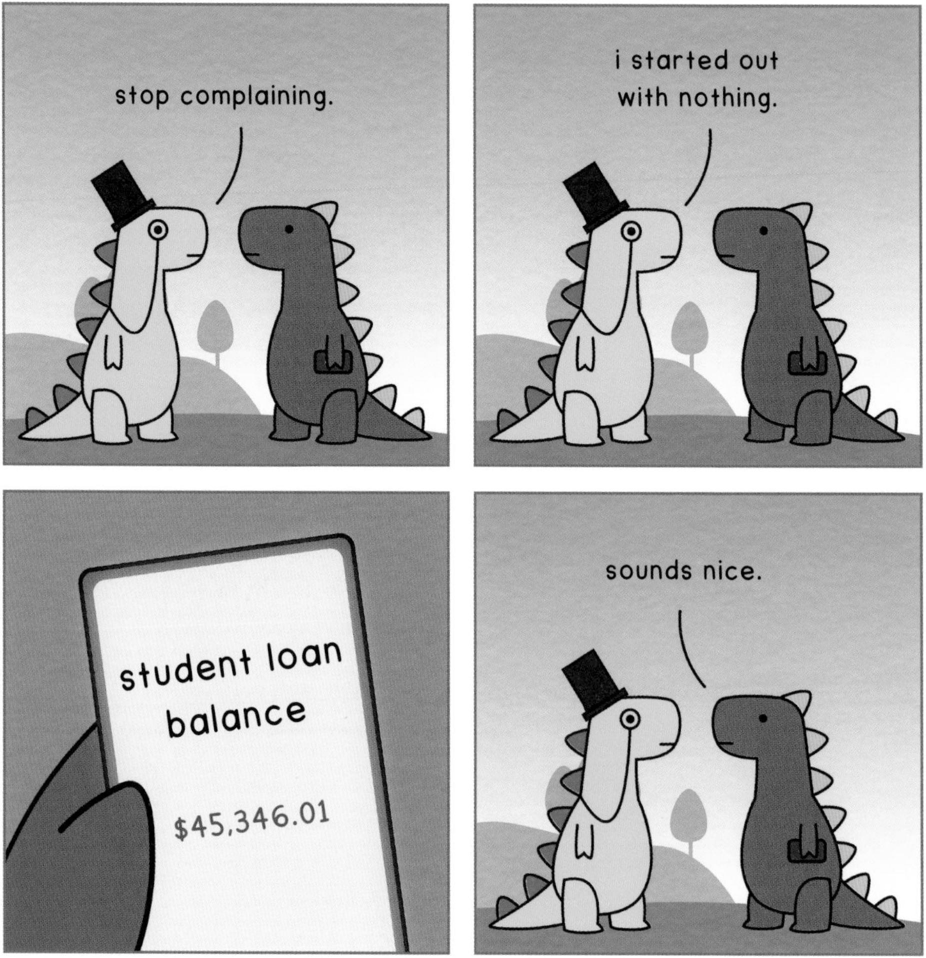
stop complaining.
i started out
with nothing.
student loan
balance
$45,346.01
sounds nice.

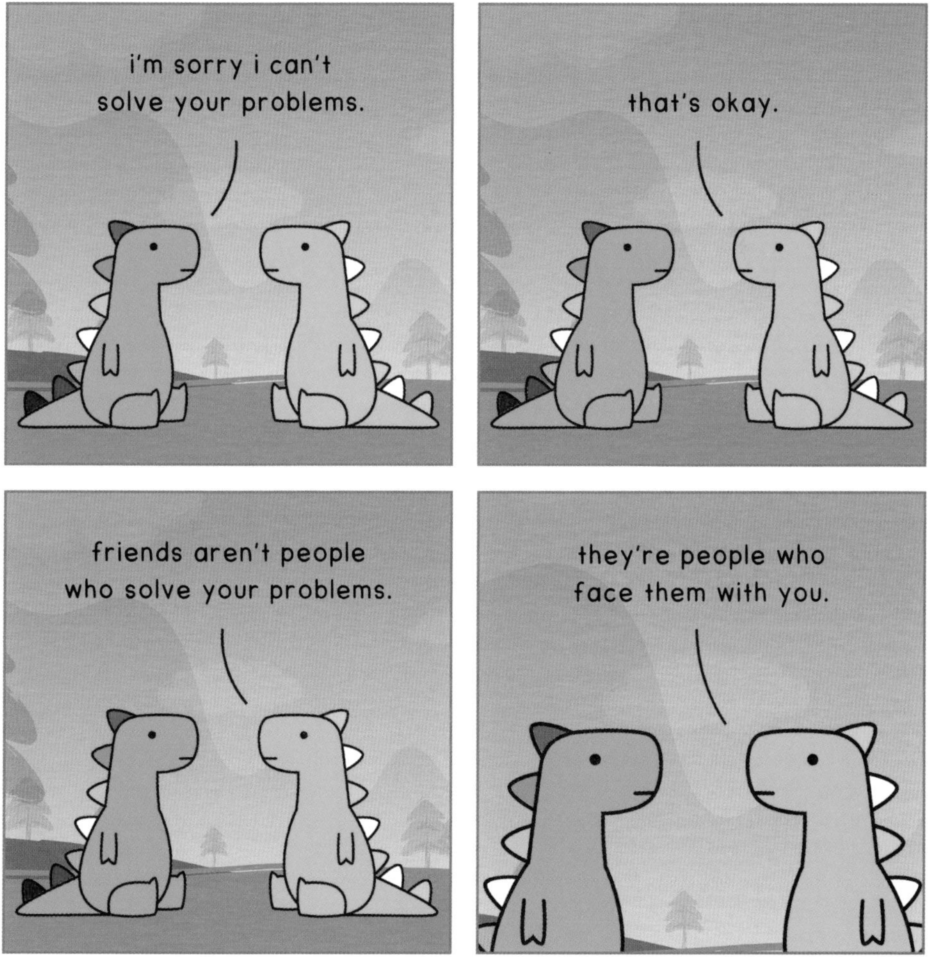
i'm sorry i can't solve your problems.
that's okay.
friends aren't people who solve your problems.
they're people who face them with you.

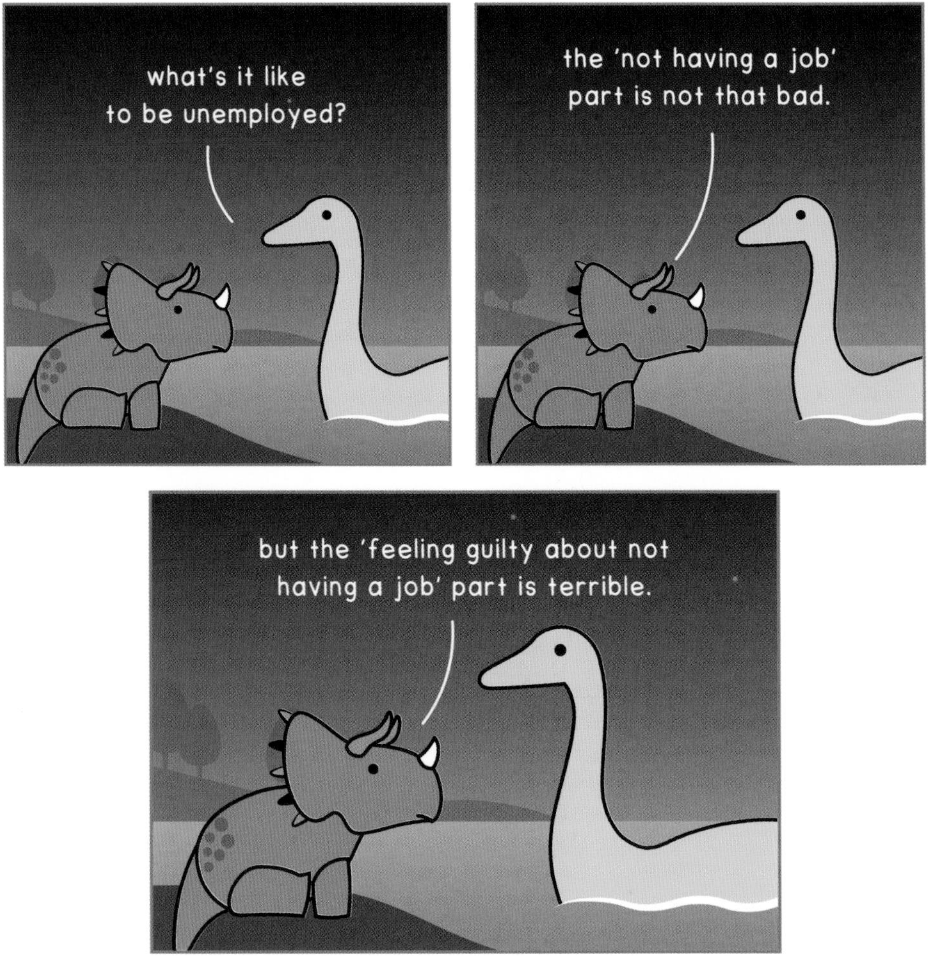
what's it like
to be unemployed?
the 'not having a job'
part is not that bad.
but the 'feeling guilty about not
having a job' part is terrible.

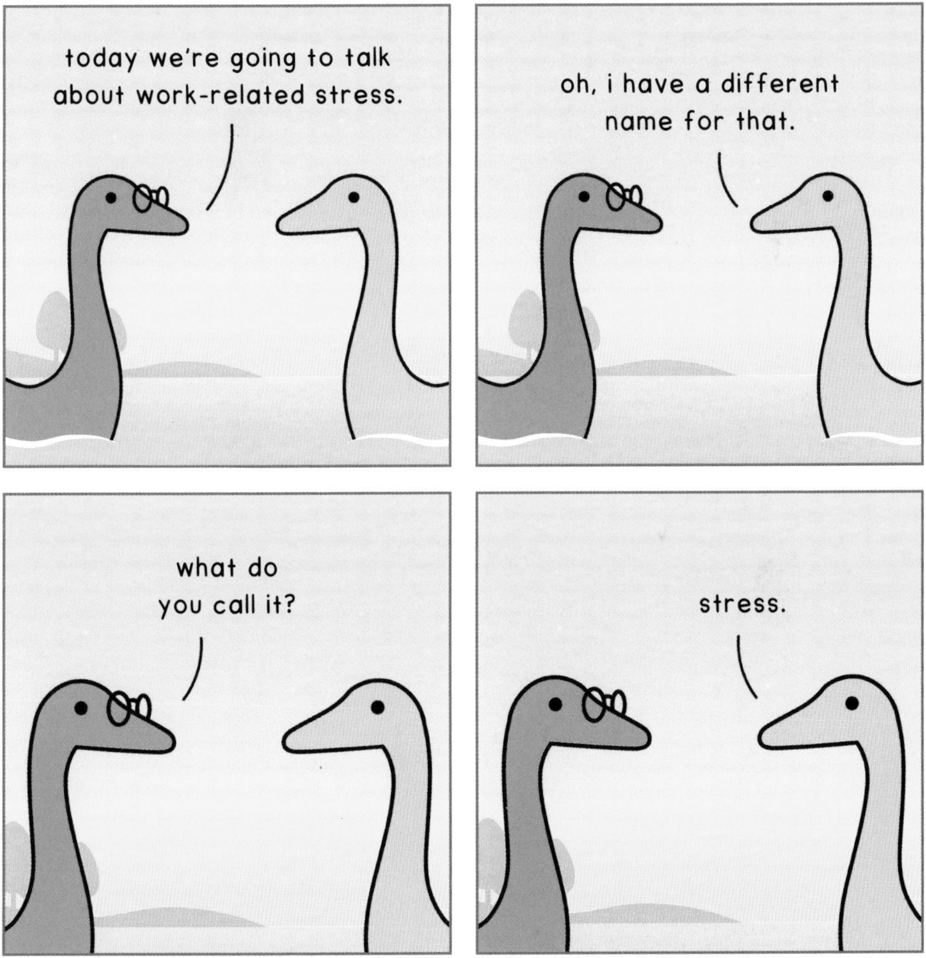
today we're going to talk about work-related stress.
oh, i have a different name for that.
what do you call it?
stress.

aesthetics

what is beauty?

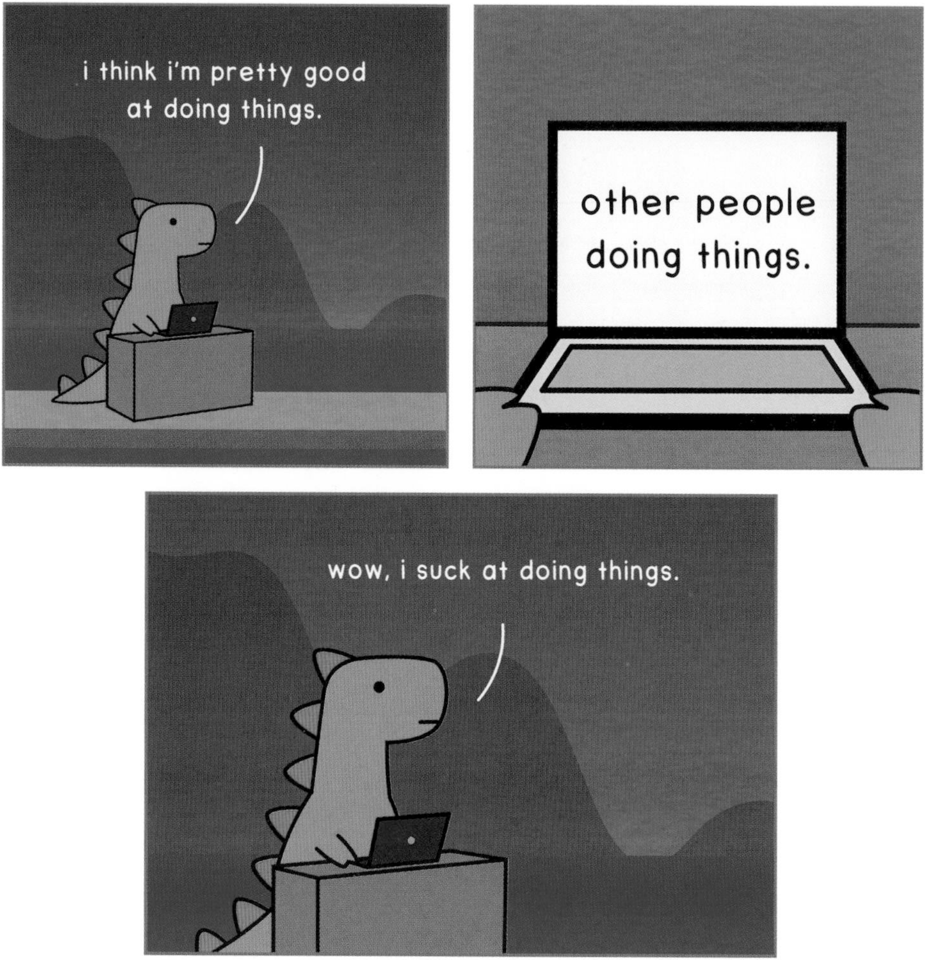
i think i'm pretty good at doing things.
other people doing things.
wow, i suck at doing things.

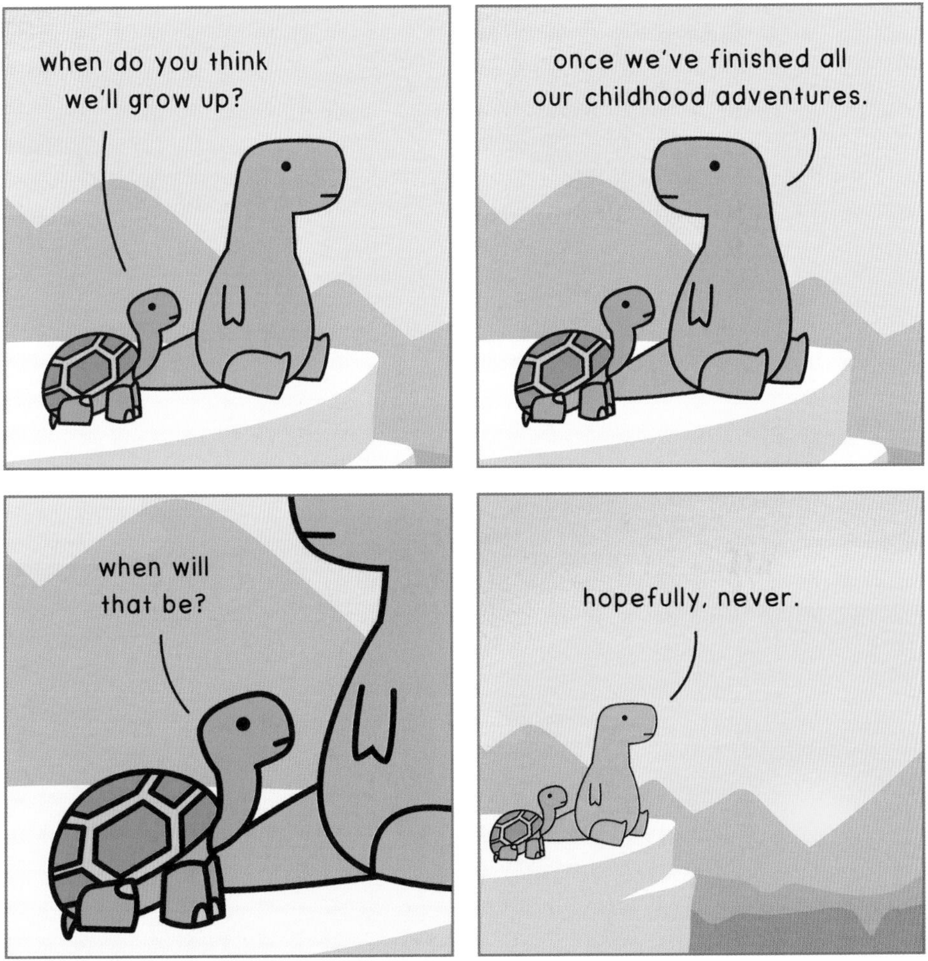
when do you think we'll grow up?
once we've finished all our childhood adventures.
when will that be?
hopefully, never.

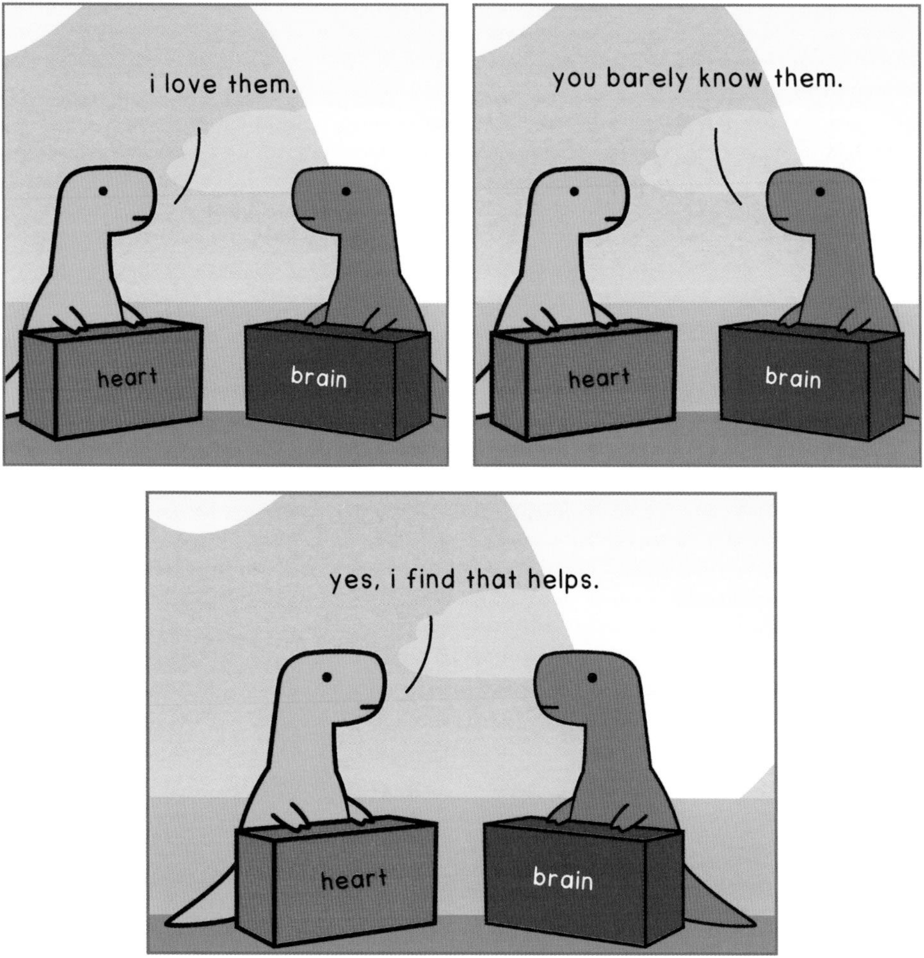
i love them.
heart
brain
you barely know them.
heart
brain
yes, i find that helps.
heart
brain

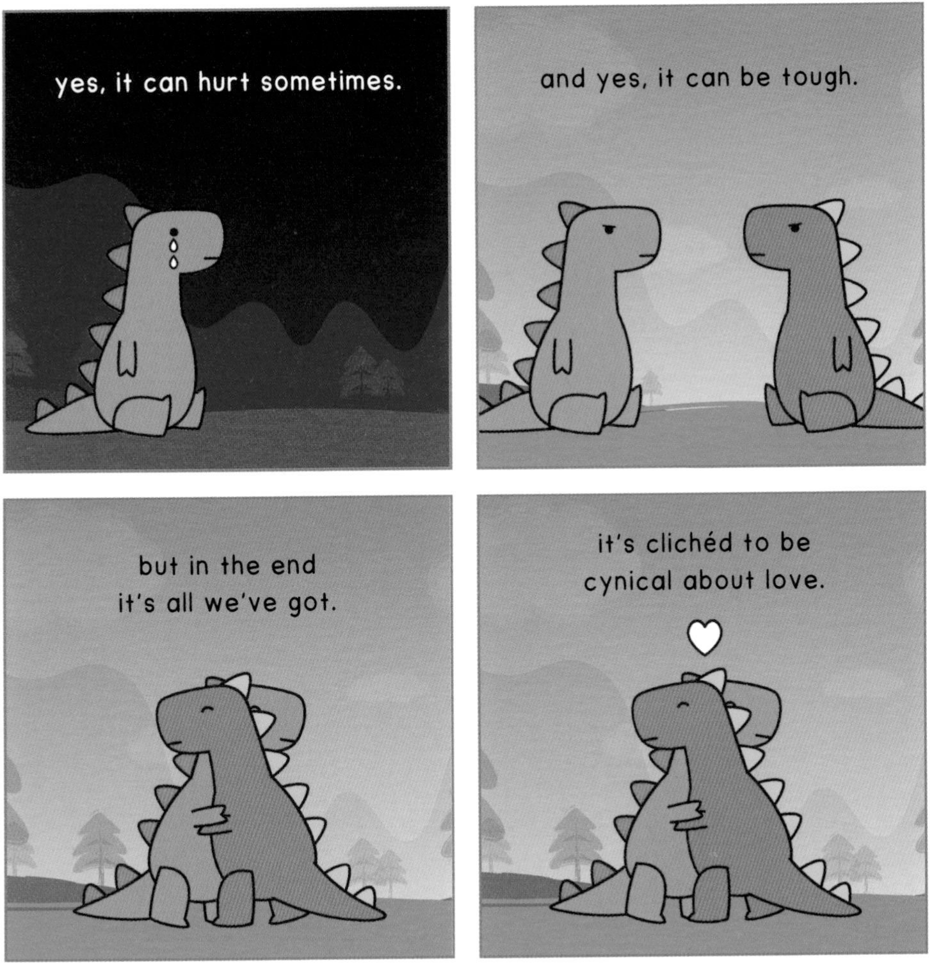
yes, it can hurt sometimes.
and yes, it can be tough.
but in the end
it's all we've got.
it's clichéd to be
cynical about love.

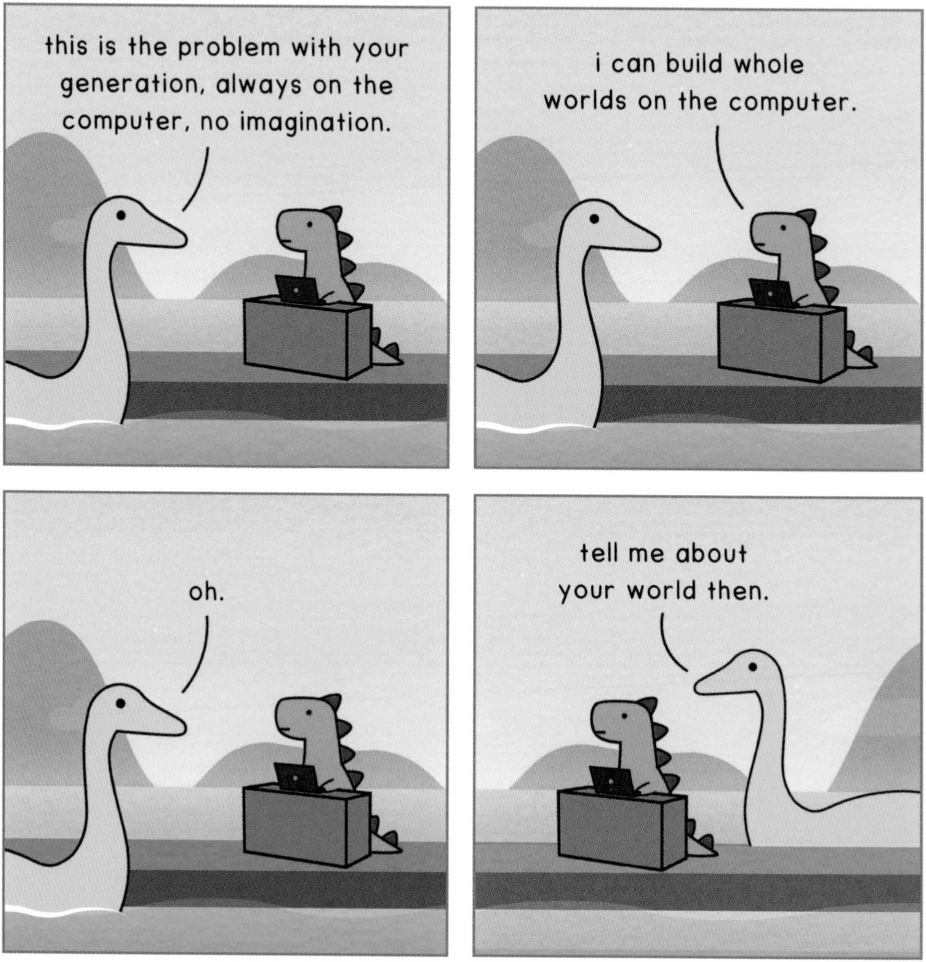
this is the problem with your generation, always on the computer, no imagination.
i can build whole worlds on the computer.
oh.
tell me about your world then.

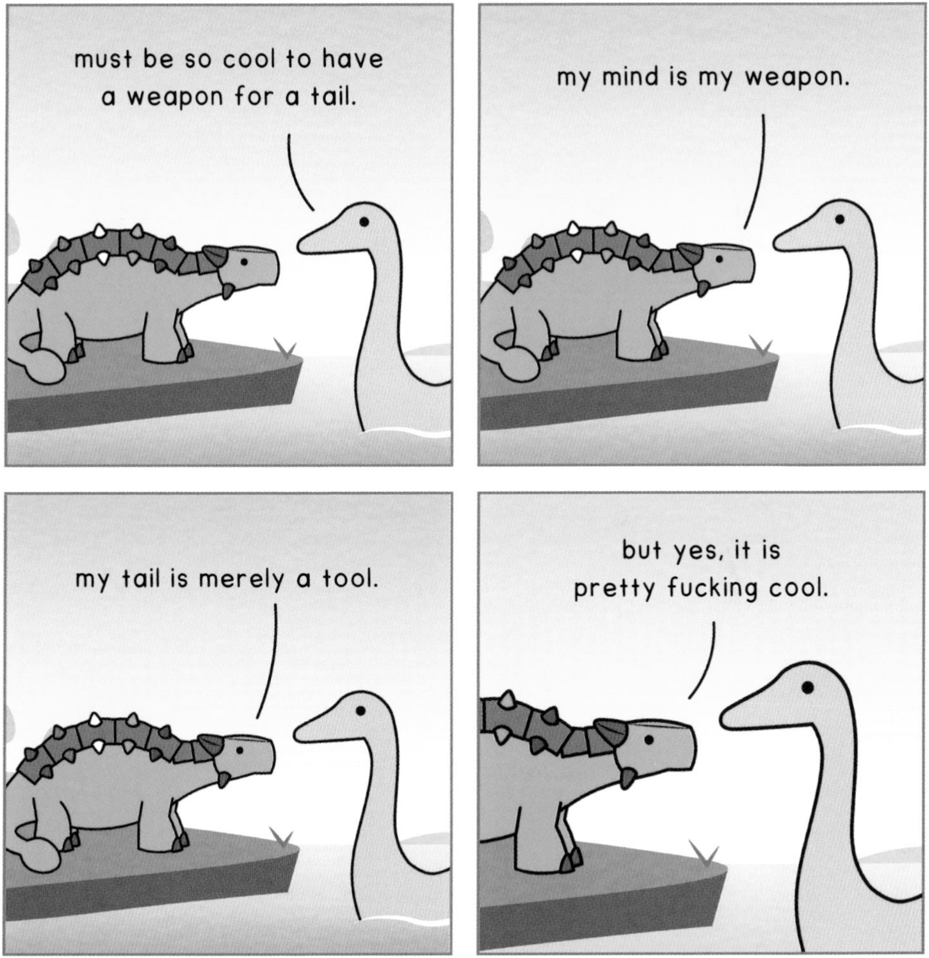
must be so cool to have
a weapon for a tail.
my mind is my weapon.
my tail is merely a tool.
but yes, it is
pretty fucking cool.

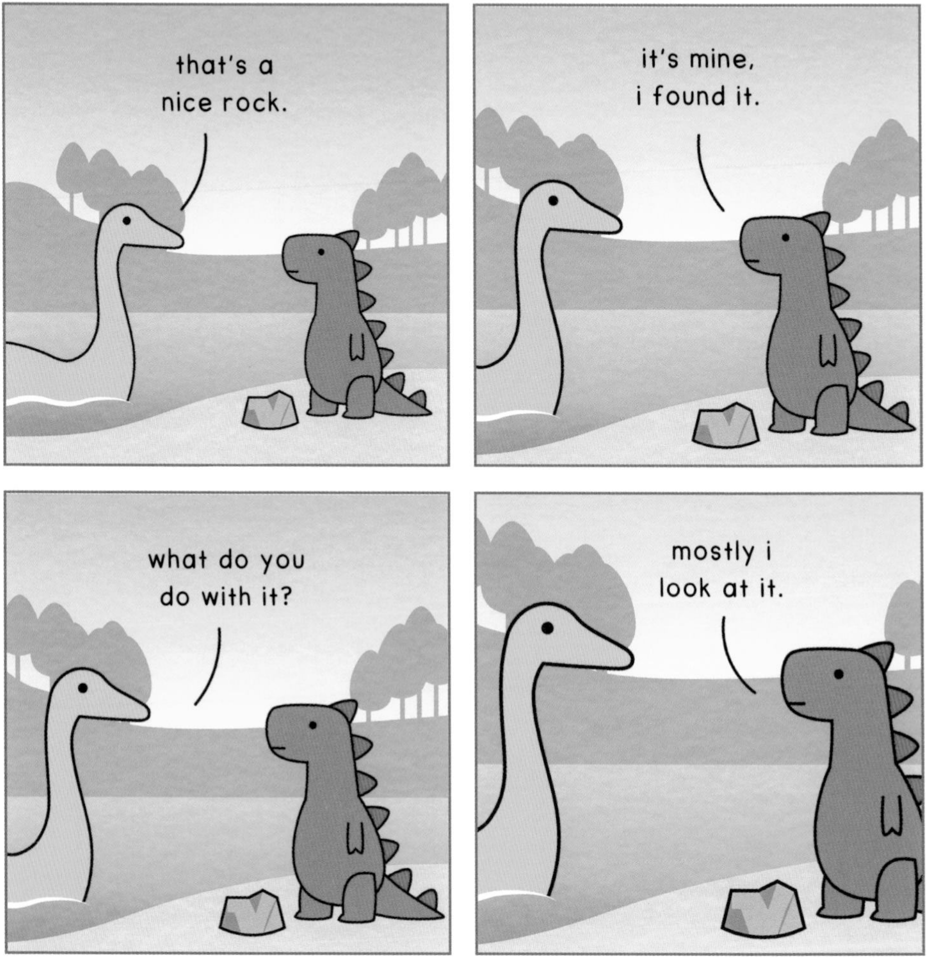
that's a nice rock.
it's mine, i found it.
what do you do with it?
mostly i look at it.

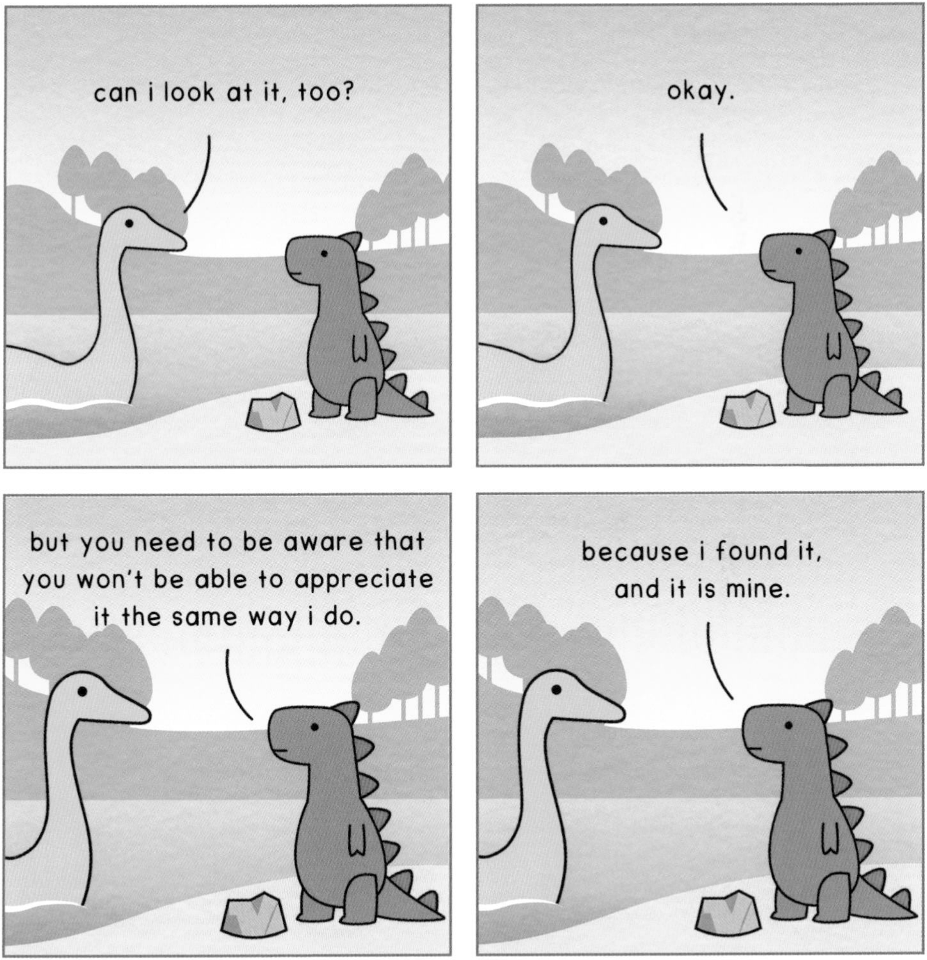
can i look at it, too?
okay.
but you need to be aware that you won't be able to appreciate it the same way i do.
because i found it, and it is mine.

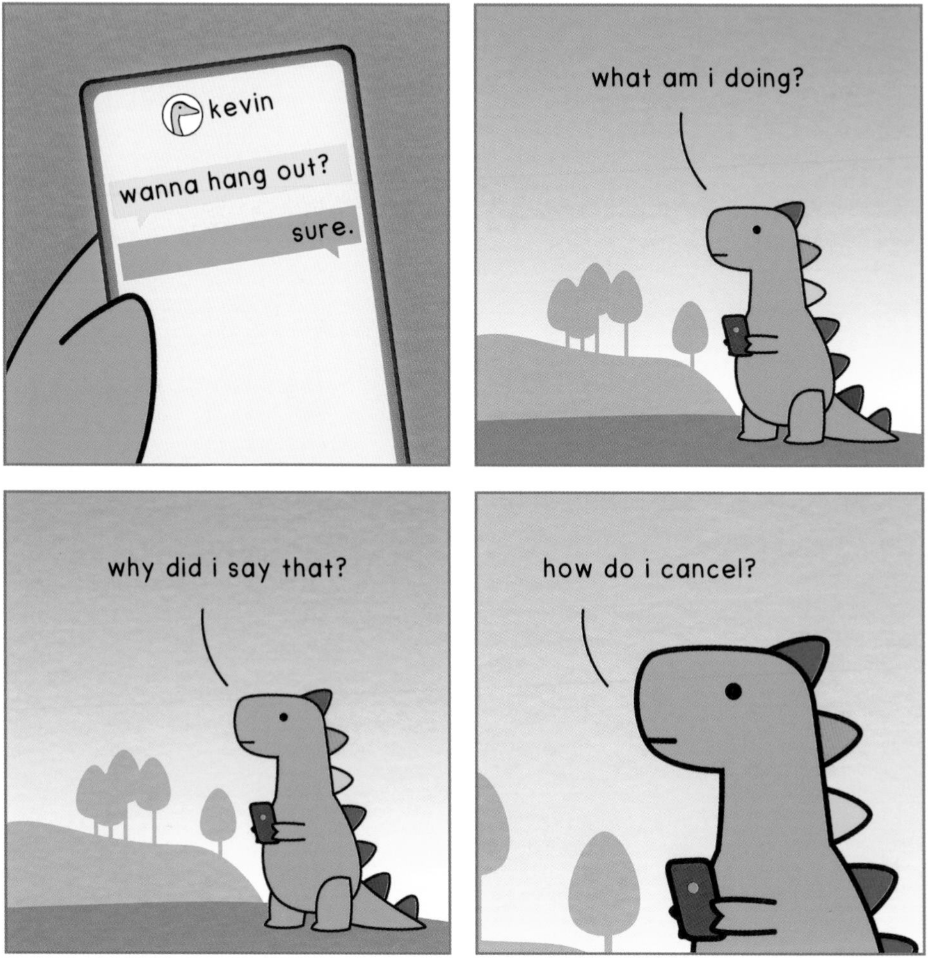
kevin
wanna hang out?
sure.
what am i doing?
why did i say that?
how do i cancel?

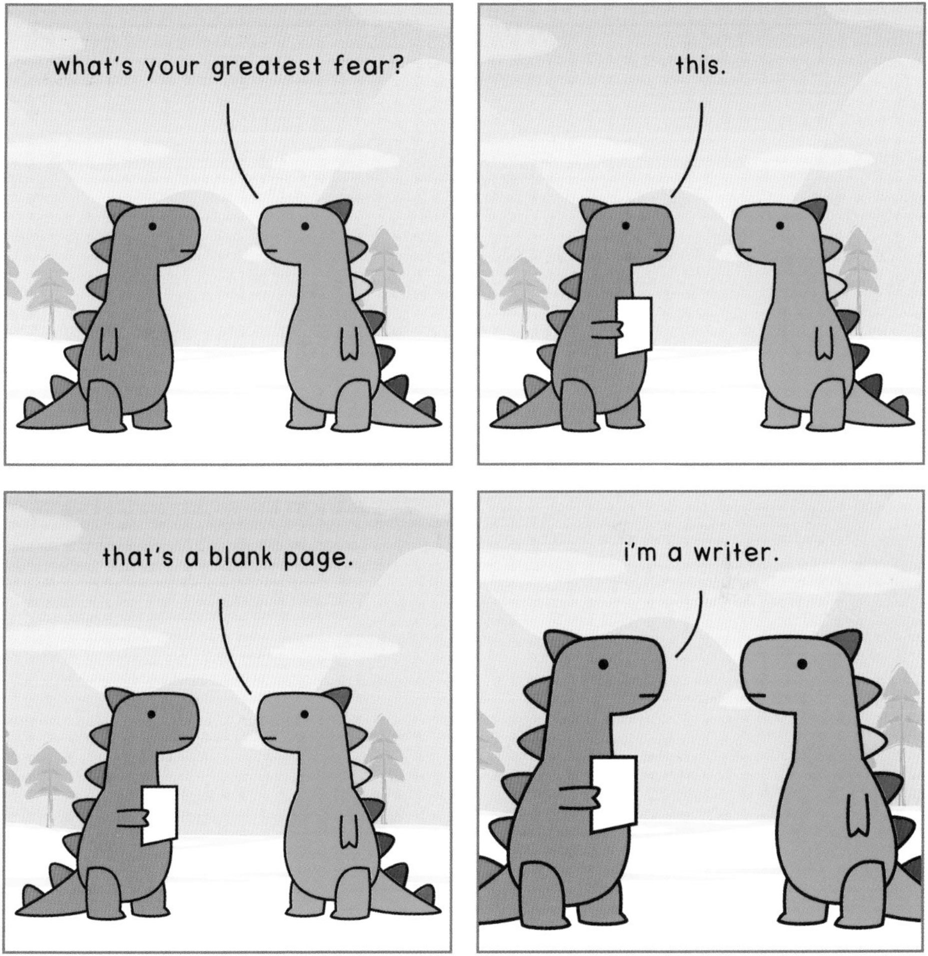
what's your greatest fear?
this.
that's a blank page.
i'm a writer.

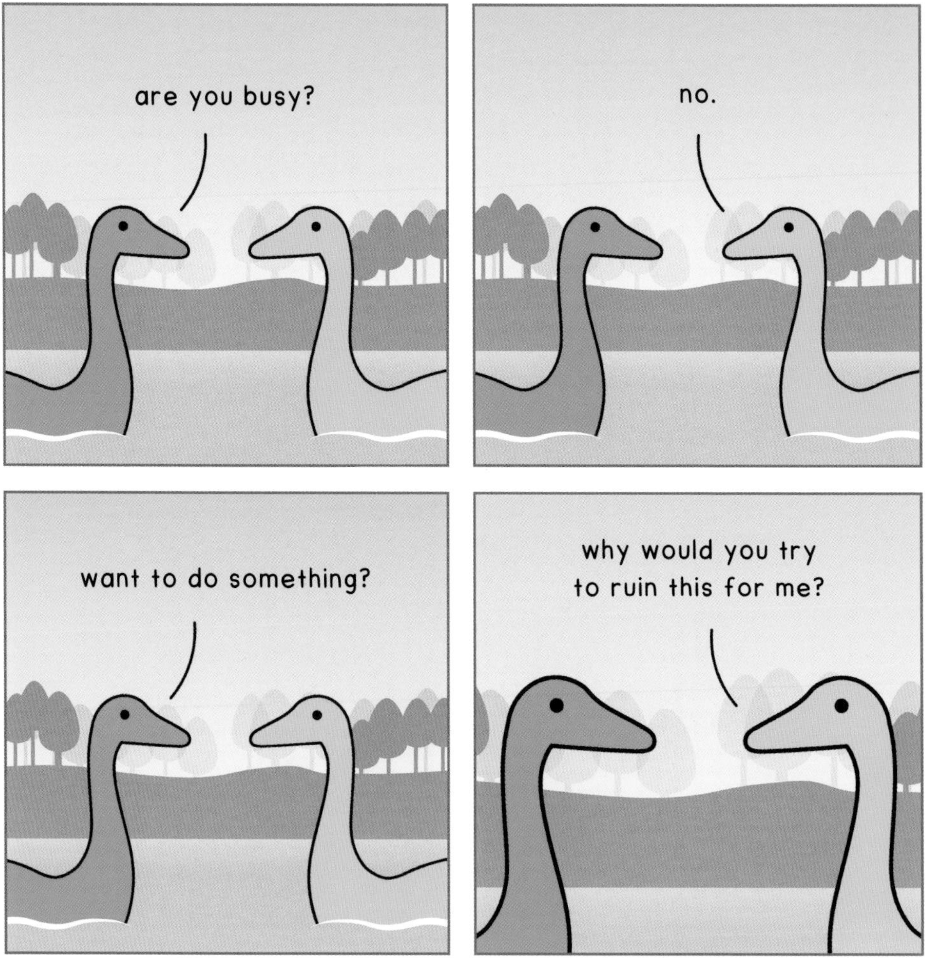
are you busy?
no.
want to do something?
why would you try to ruin this for me?

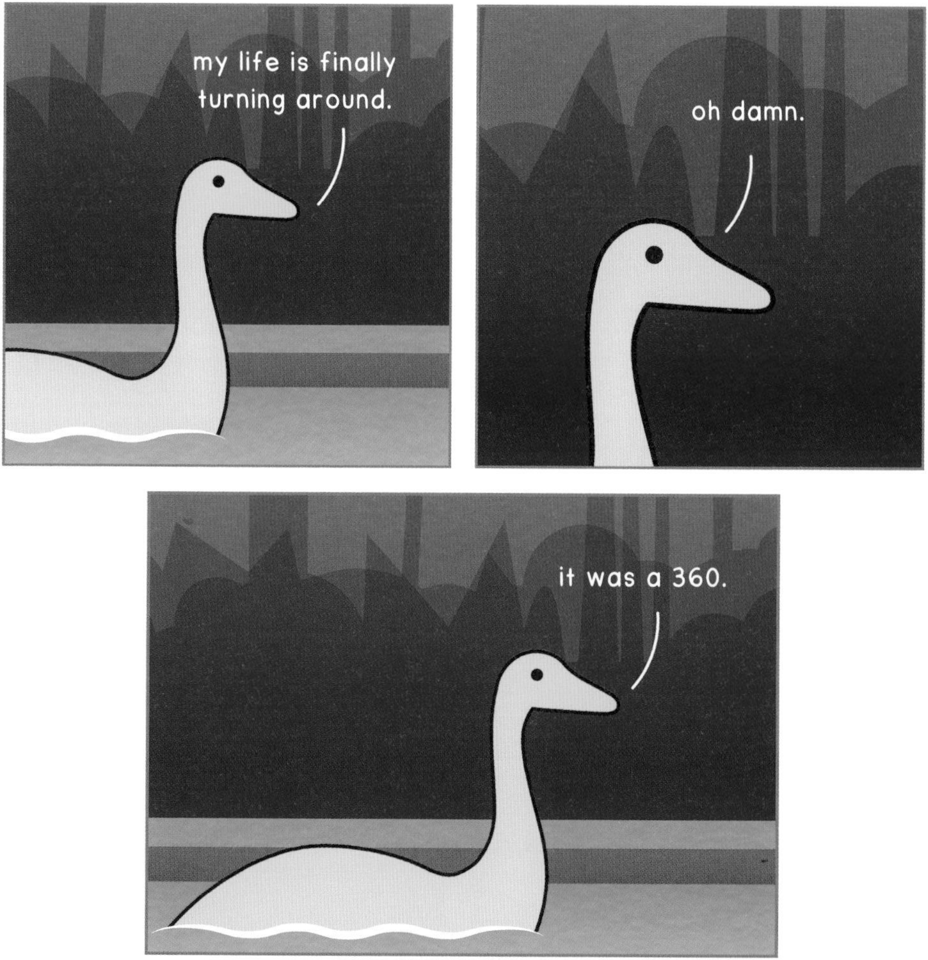
my life is finally turning around.
oh damn.
it was a 360.

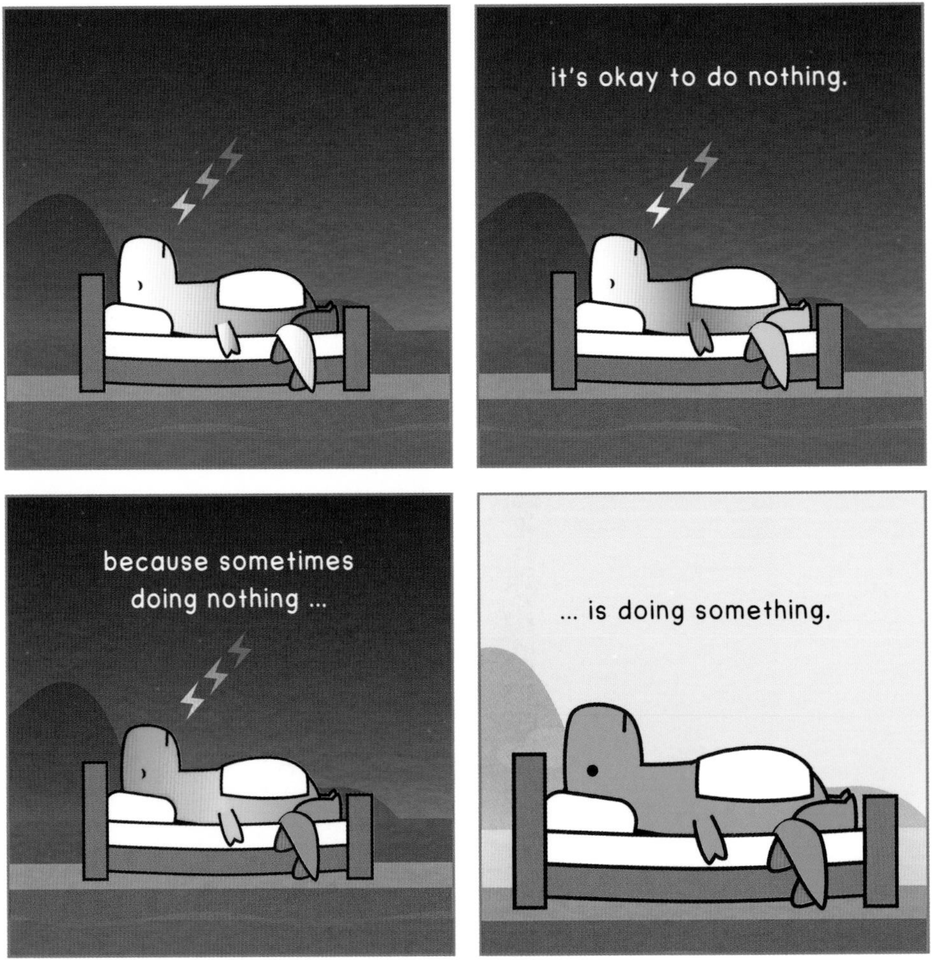
it's okay to do nothing.
because sometimes doing nothing ...
... is doing something.

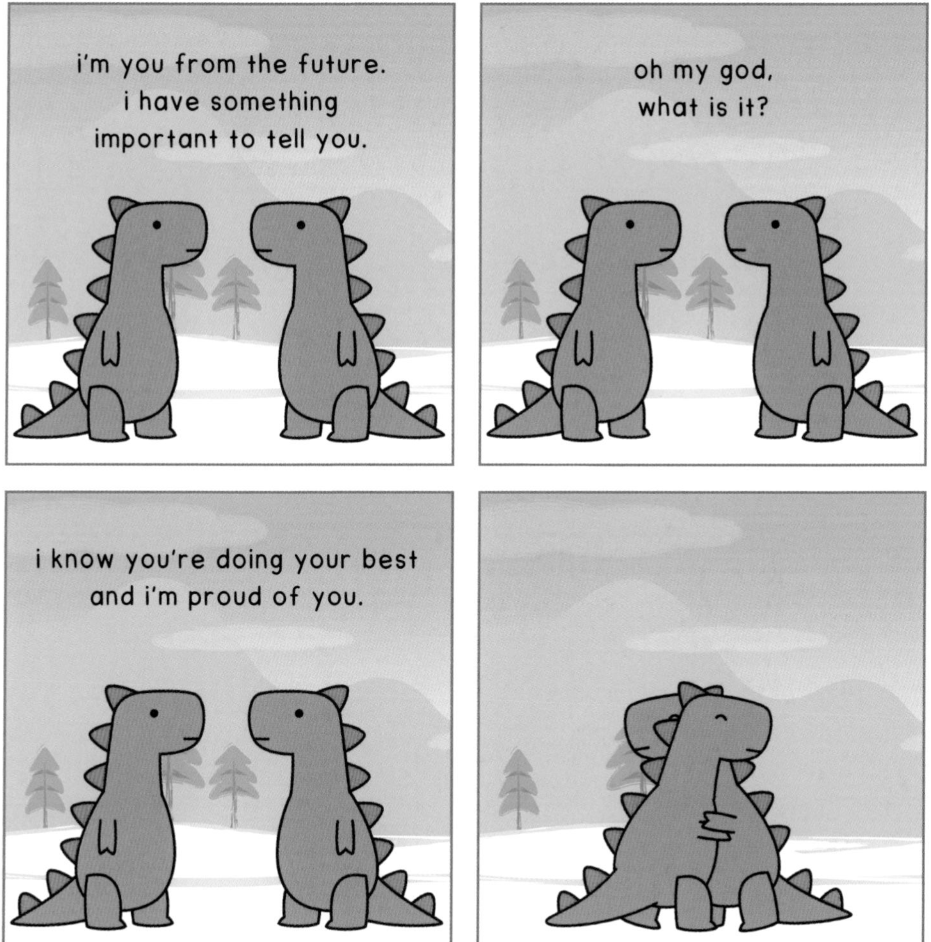
i'm you from the future.
i have something
important to tell you.
oh my god,
what is it?
i know you're doing your best
and i'm proud of you.

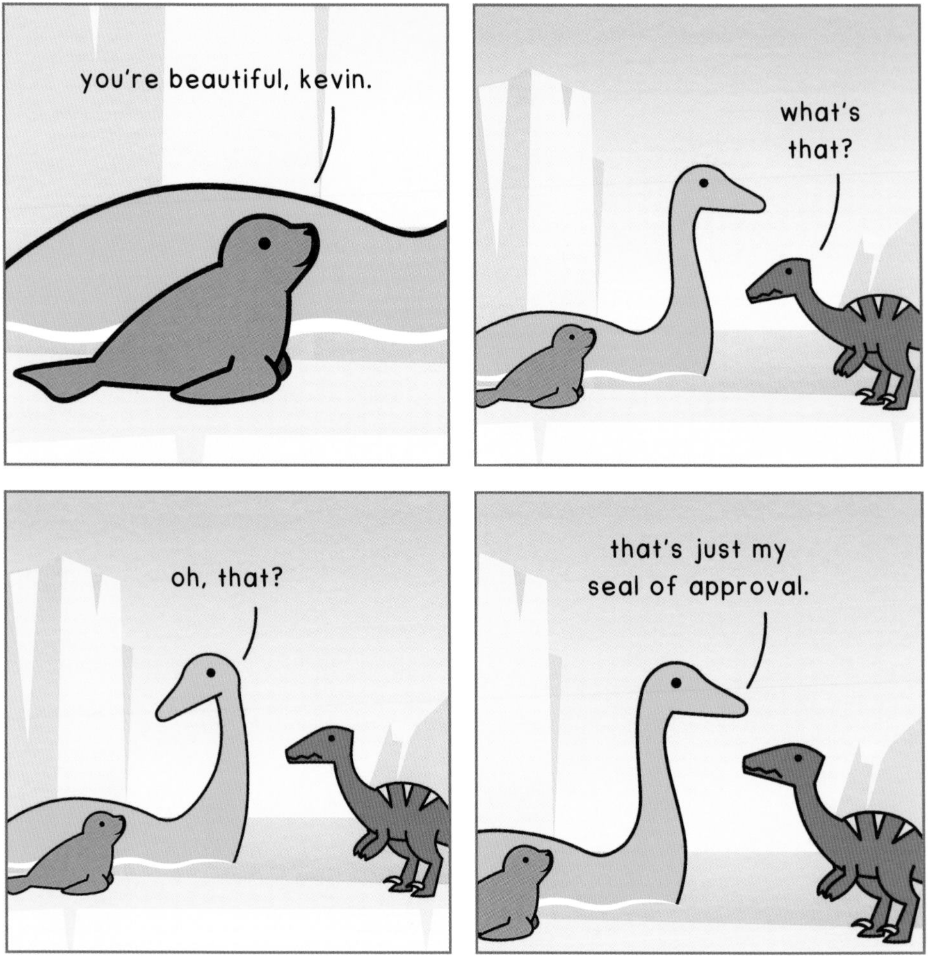
you're beautiful, kevin.
what's that?
oh, that?
that's just my seal of approval.

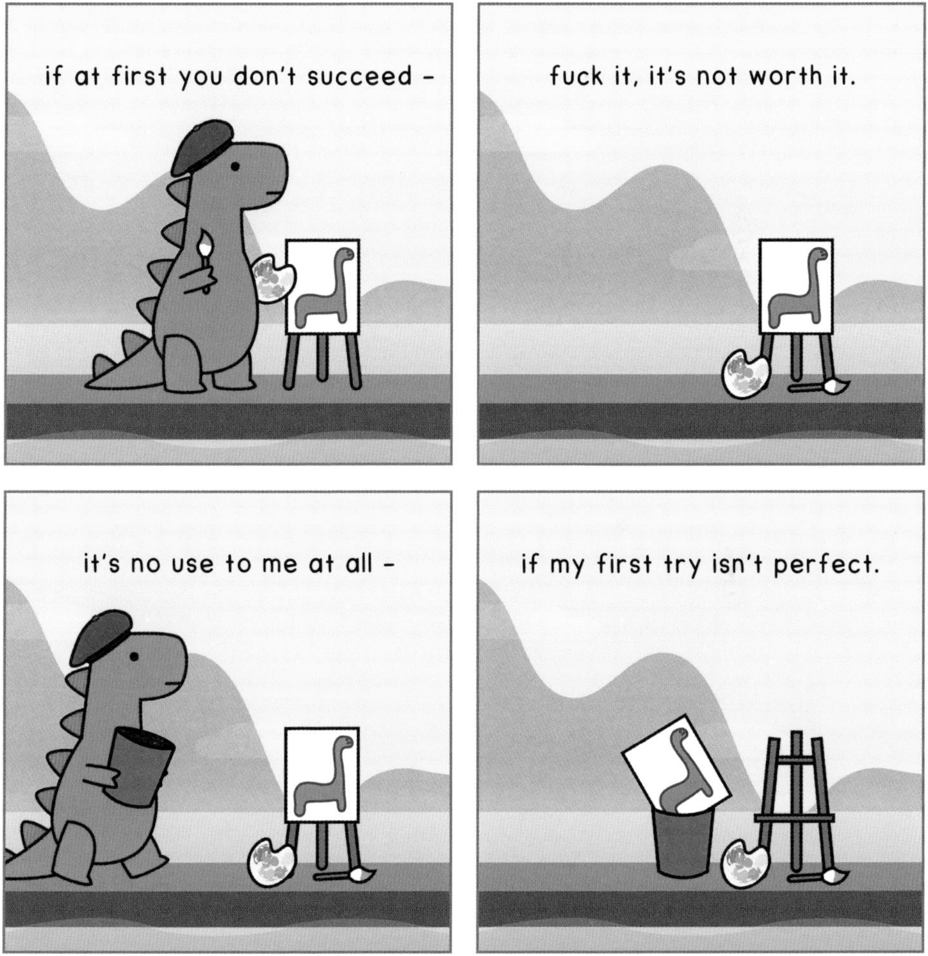
if at first you don't succeed -
fuck it, it's not worth it.
it's no use to me at all -
if my first try isn't perfect.

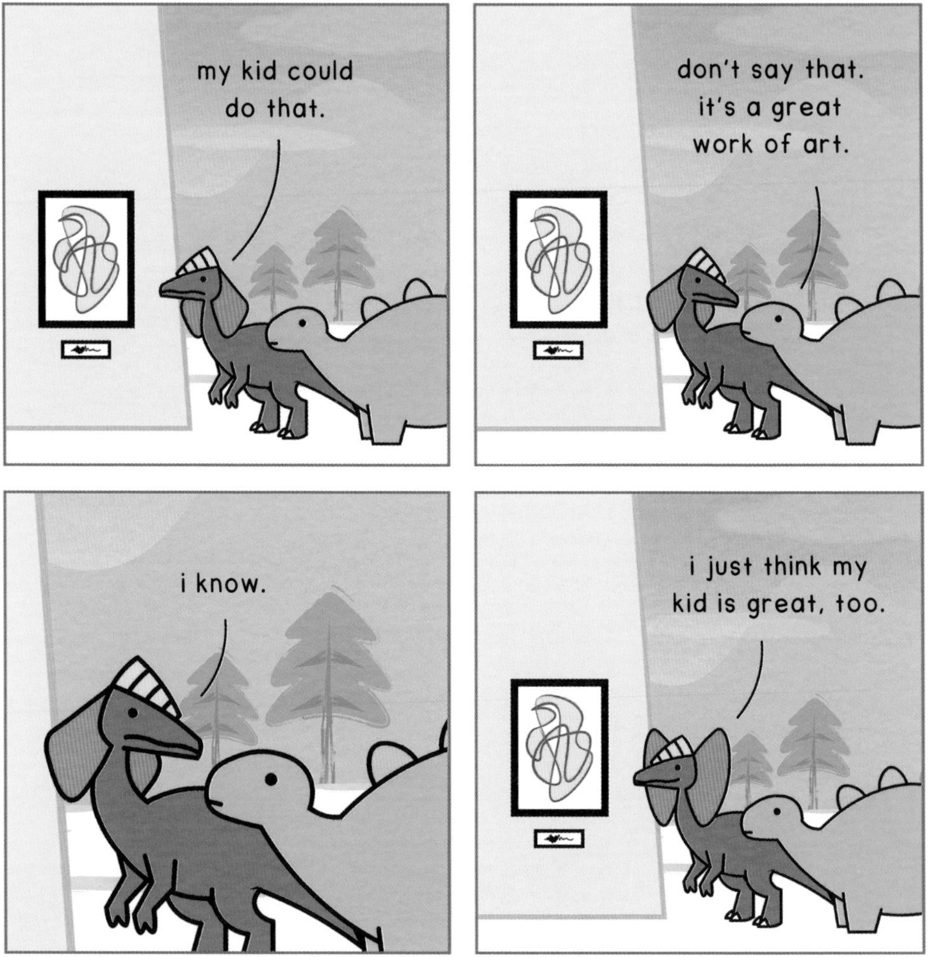
my kid could do that.
don't say that. it's a great work of art.
i know.
i just think my kid is great, too.

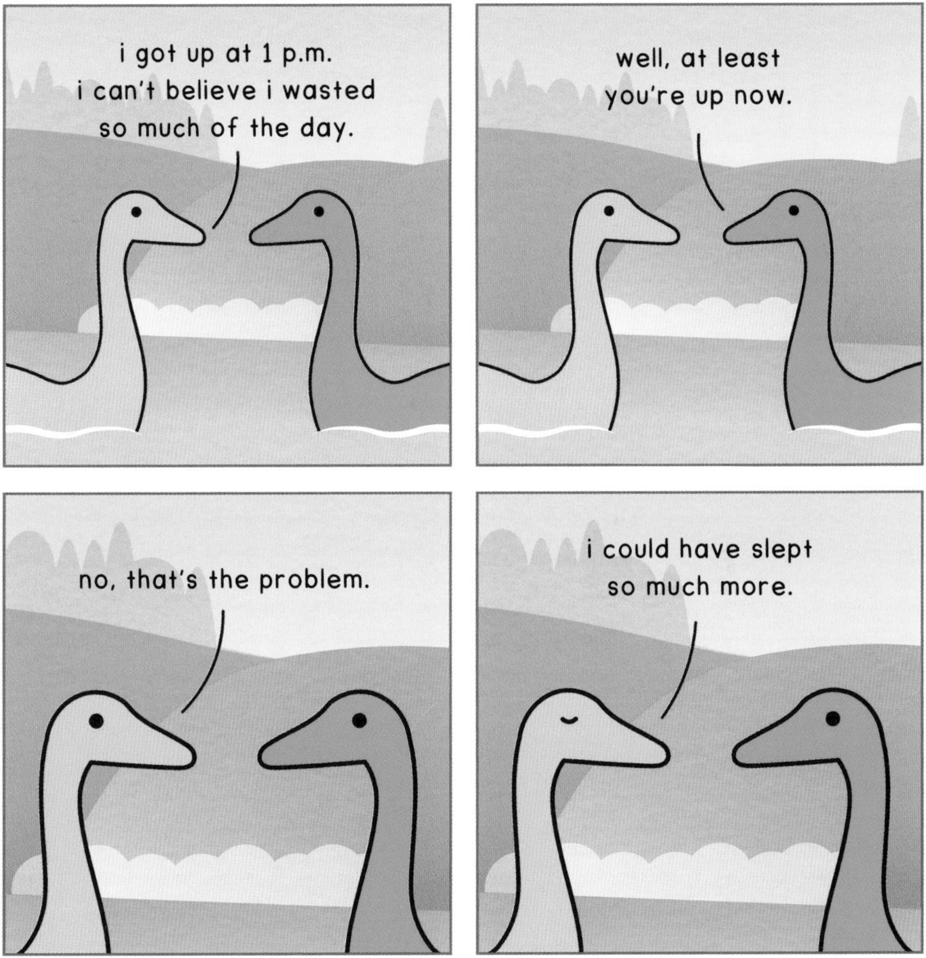
i got up at 1 p.m.
i can't believe i wasted
so much of the day.
well, at least
you're up now.
no, that's the problem.
i could have slept
so much more.

free thinking

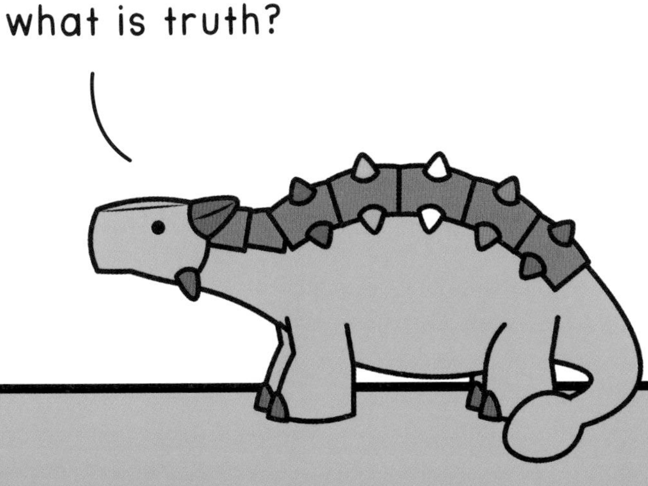
what is truth?

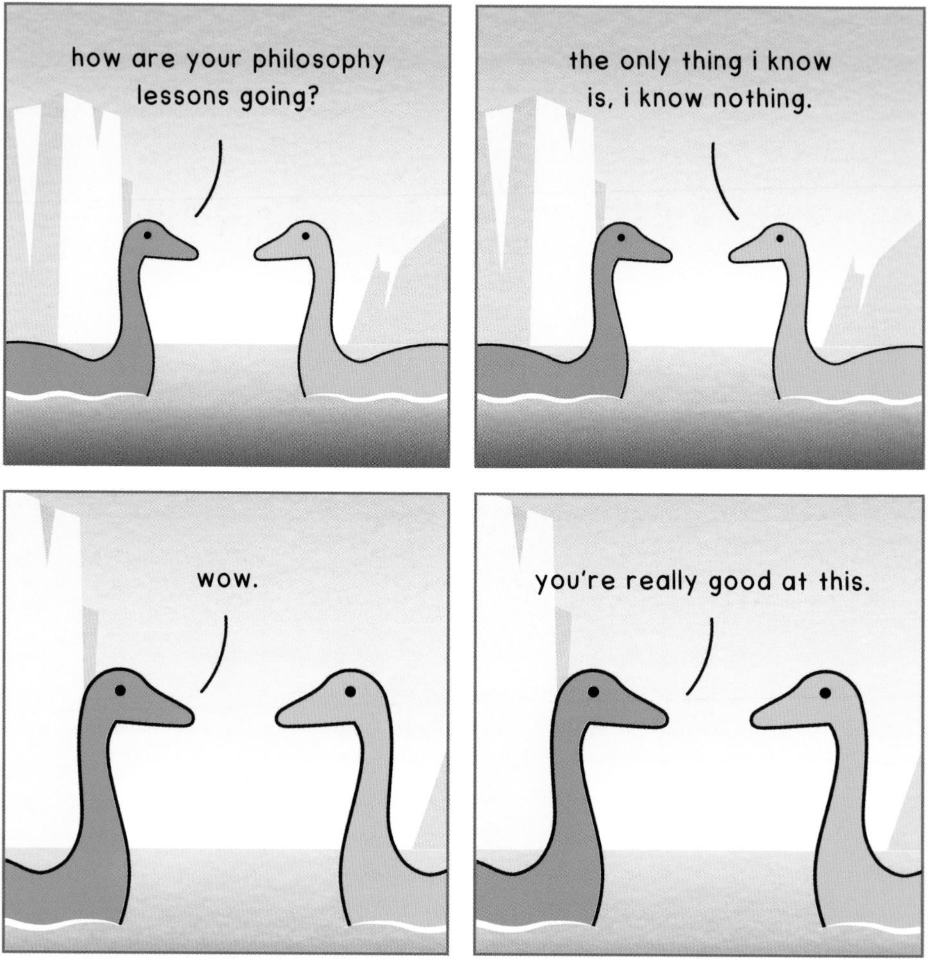
how are your philosophy lessons going?
the only thing i know is, i know nothing.
wow.
you're really good at this.

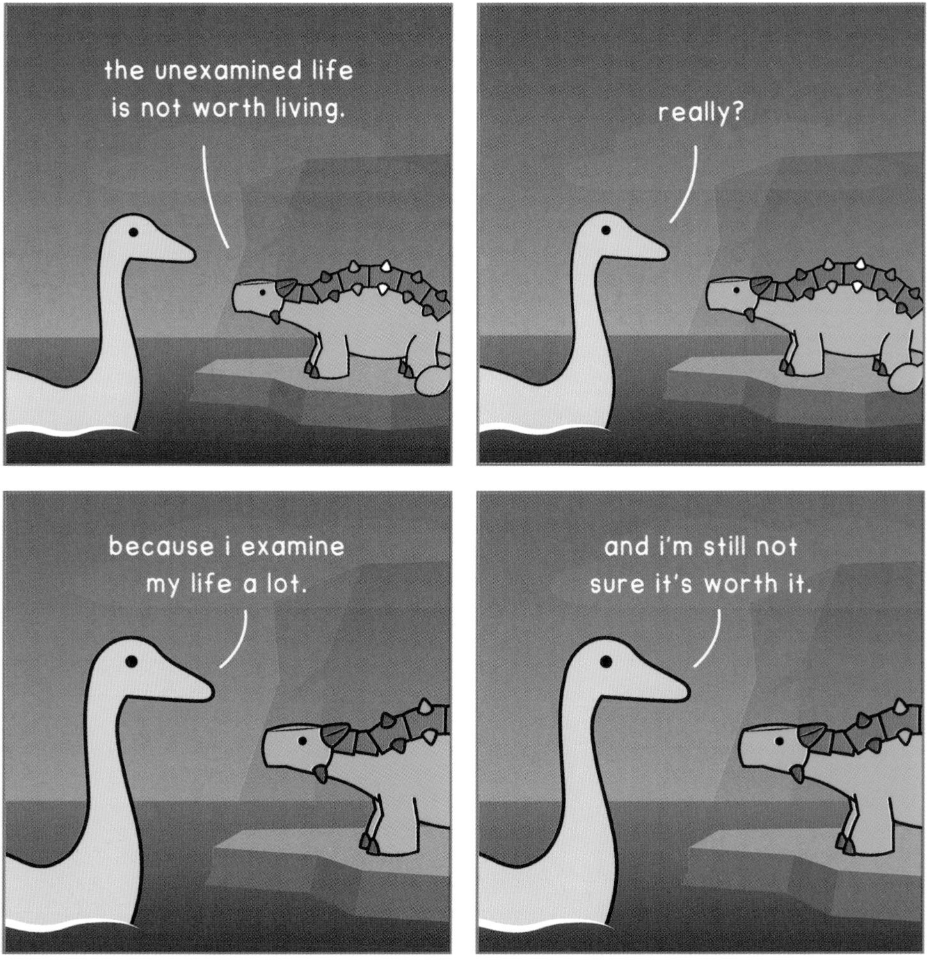
the unexamined life is not worth living.
really?
because i examine my life a lot.
and i'm still not sure it's worth it.

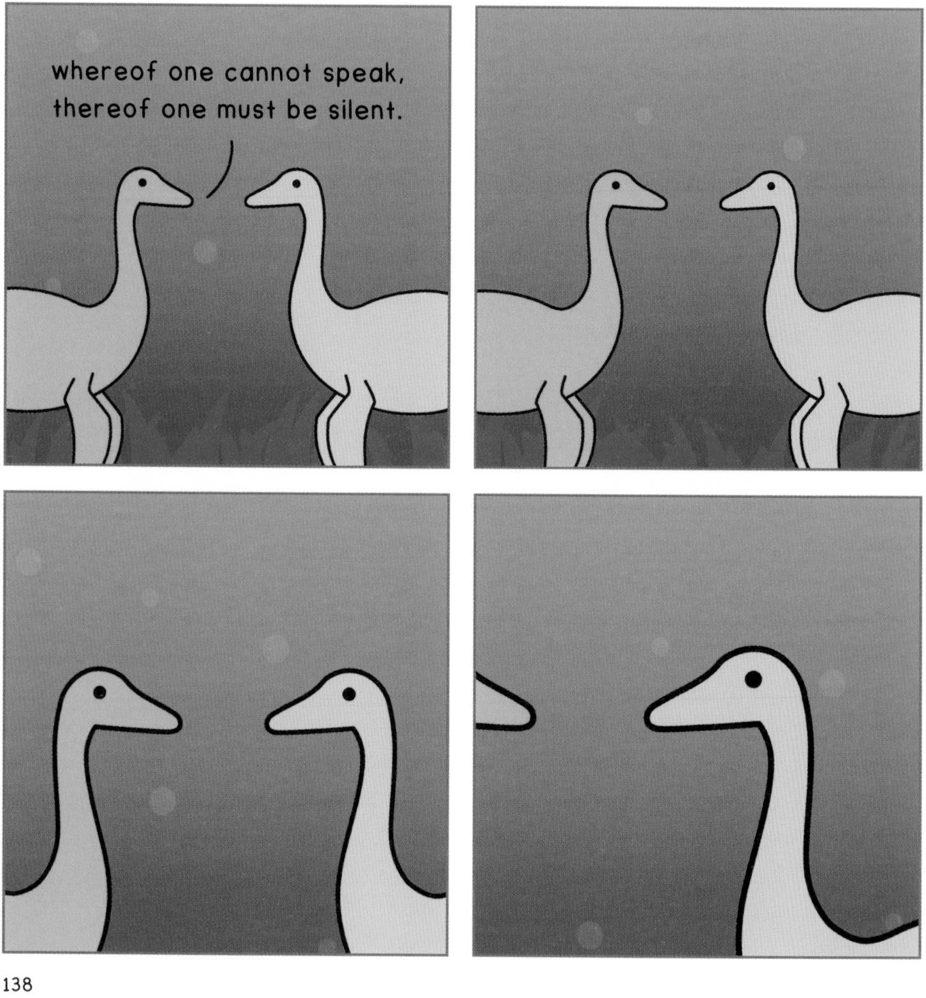
whereof one cannot speak,
thereof one must be silent.

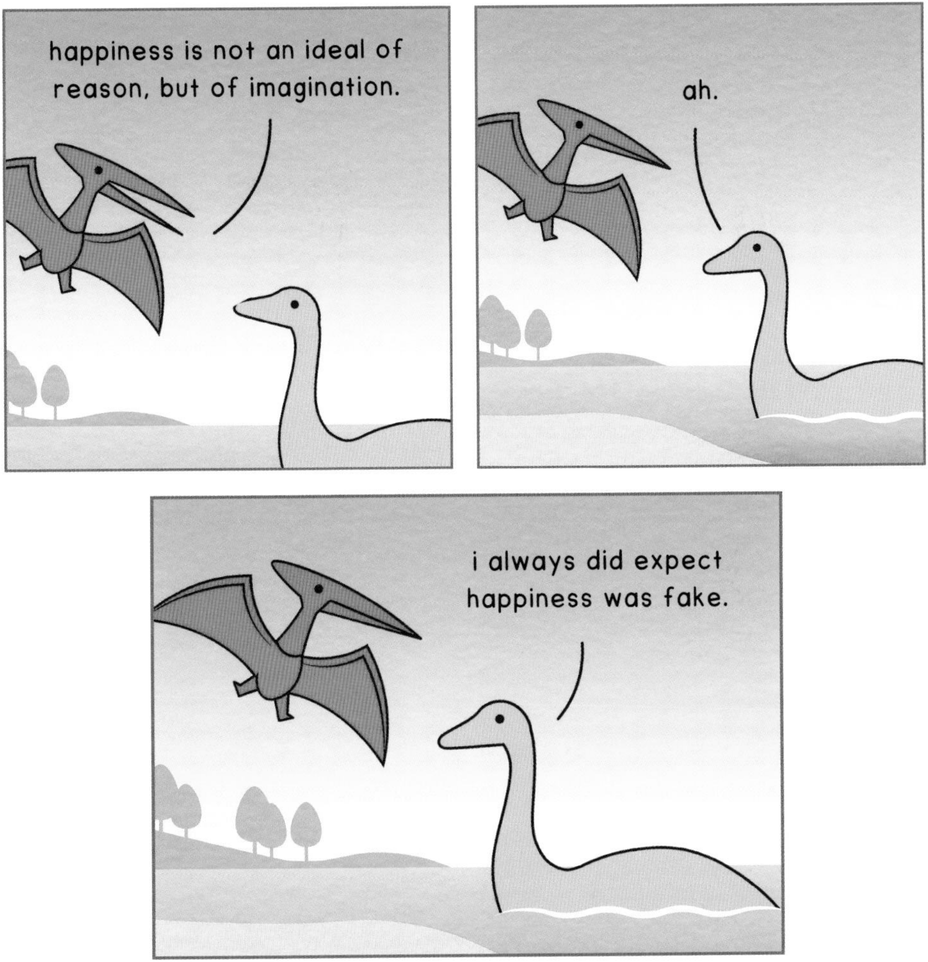
happiness is not an ideal of reason, but of imagination.
ah.
i always did expect happiness was fake.

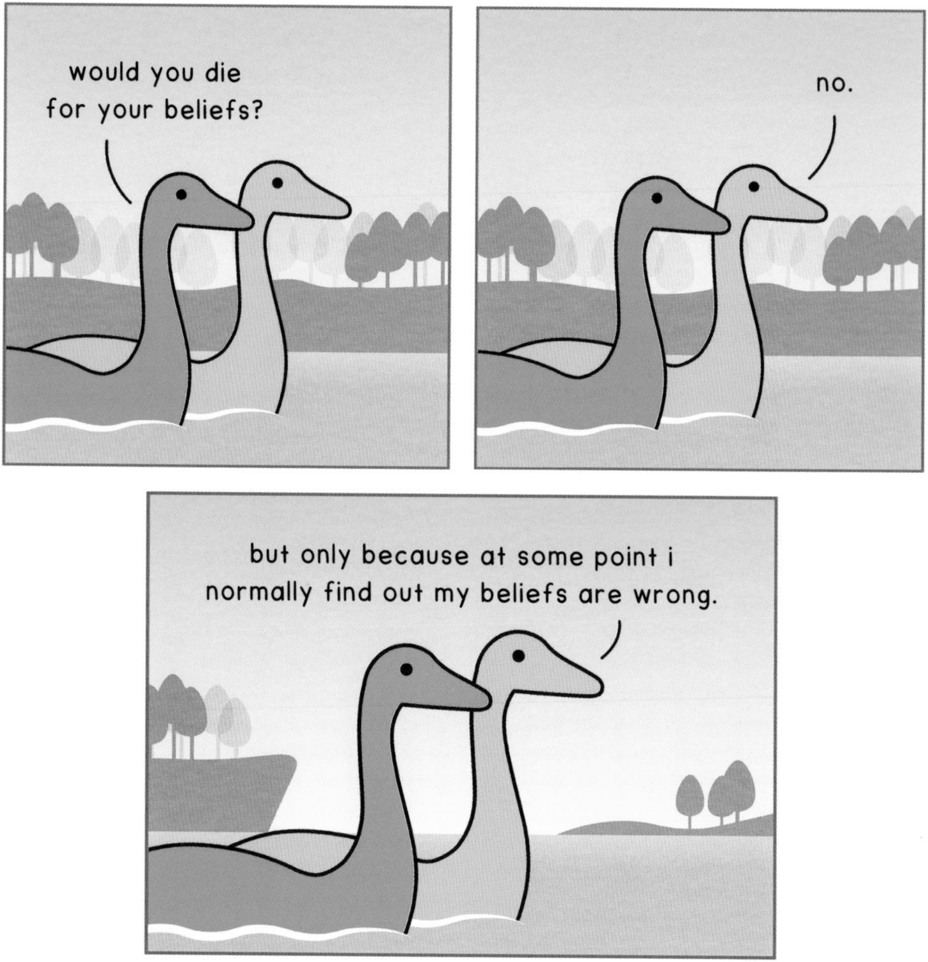
would you die
for your beliefs?
no.
but only because at some point i
normally find out my beliefs are wrong.

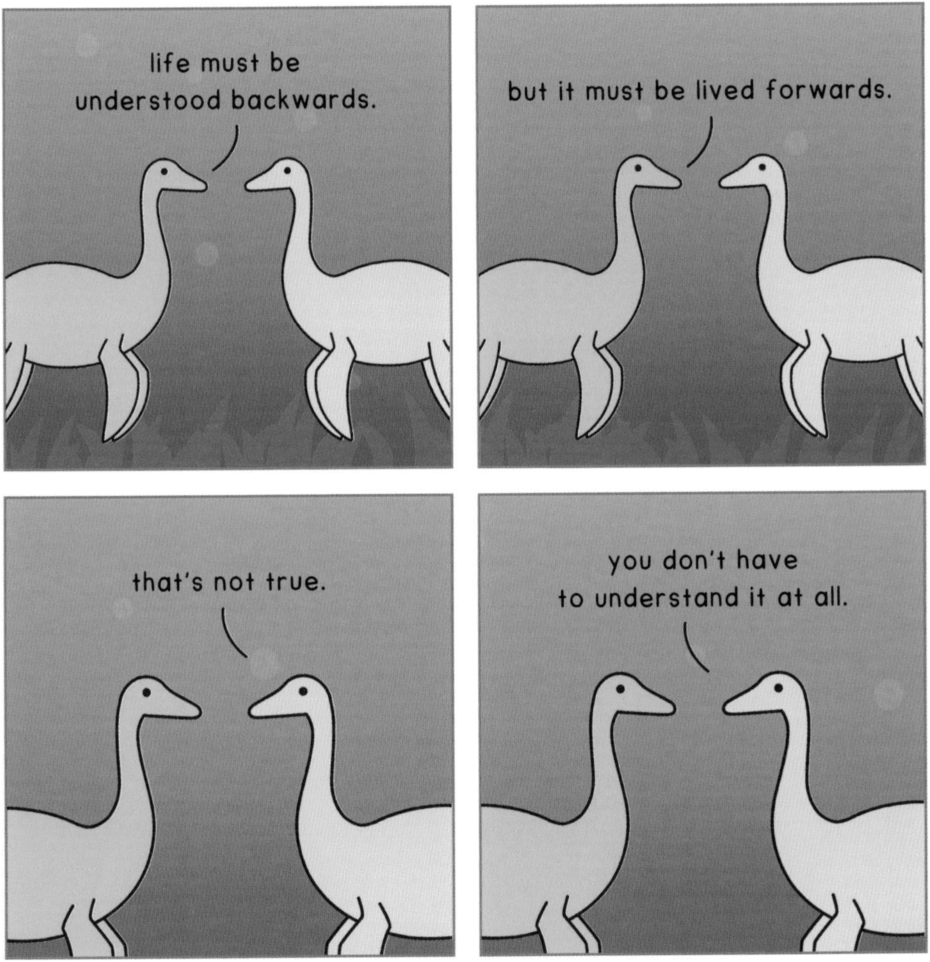
life must be understood backwards.
but it must be lived forwards.
that's not true.
you don't have to understand it at all.

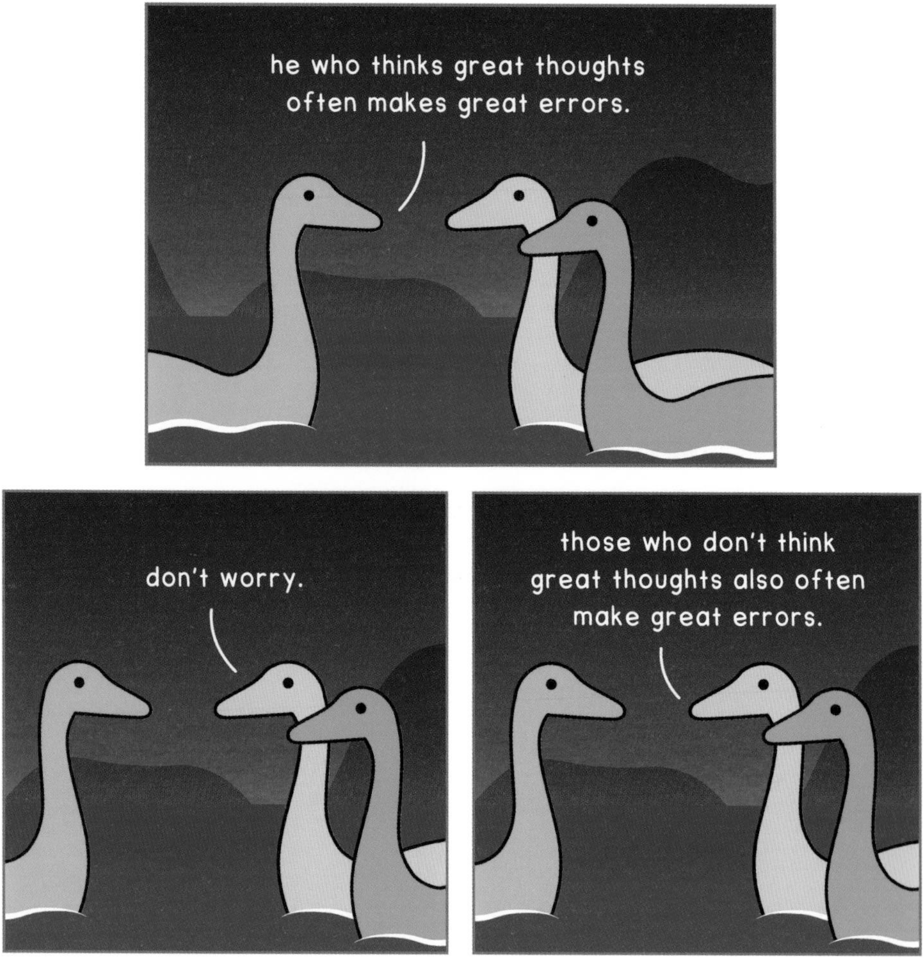
he who thinks great thoughts often makes great errors.
don't worry.
those who don't think great thoughts also often make great errors.

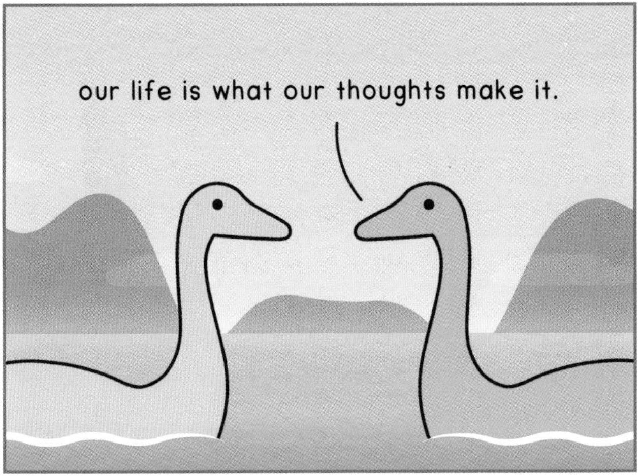
our life is what our thoughts make it.

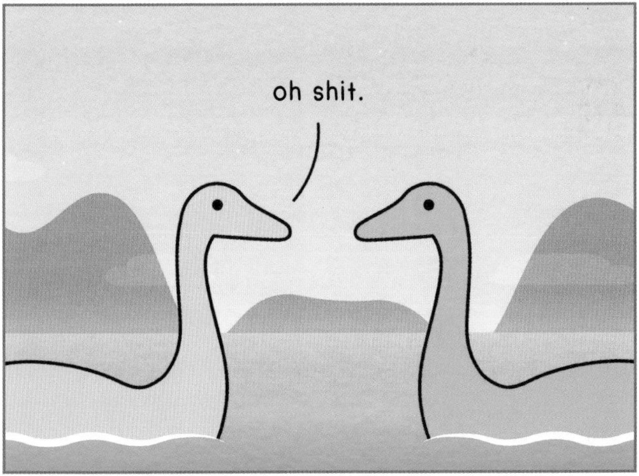
oh shit.

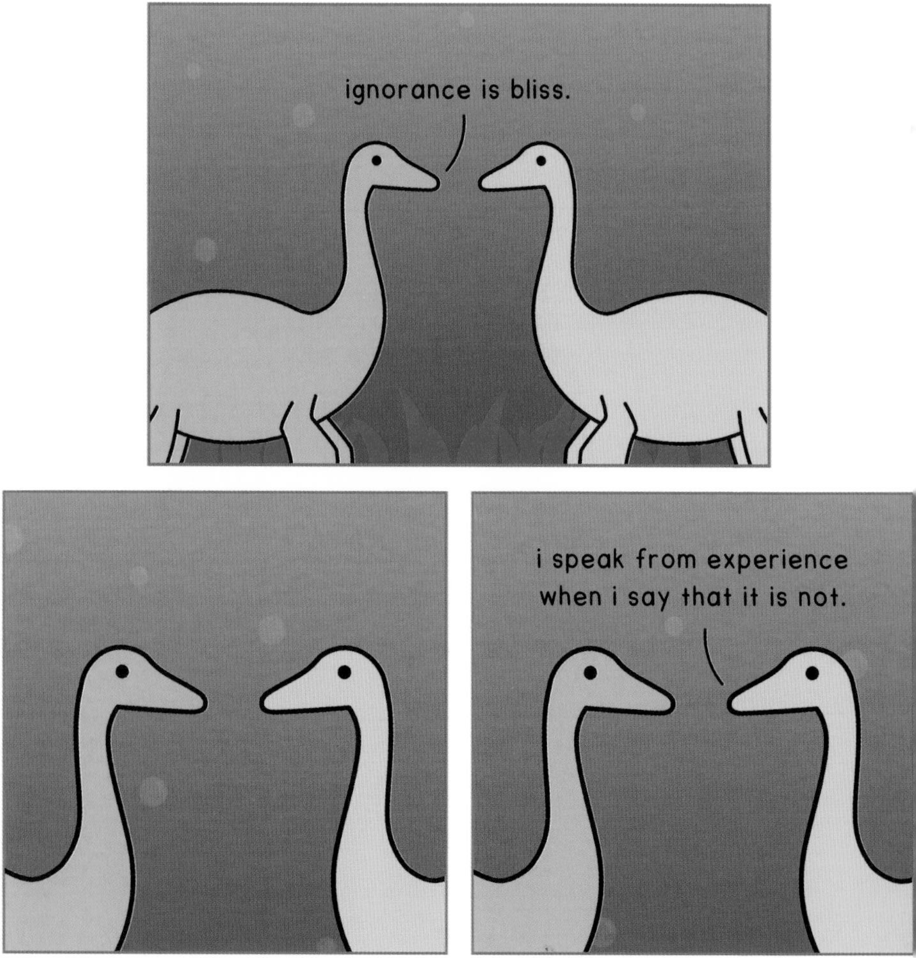
ignorance is bliss.
i speak from experience
when i say that it is not.